CELEBRATING MARRIAGE

Preparing the Wedding Liturgy
A Workbook for Engaged Couples

PAUL COVINO, Editor
Lawrence Madden
Elaine Rendler
John Buscemi

The Pastoral Press
Washington, D.C.

ISBN 0-912405-34-1

The Pastoral Press
225 Sheridan Street, NW
Washington, D.C. 20011
(202) 723-1254

The Pastoral Press is the Publications division of the National Association of Pastoral Musicians, a membership organization of musicians and clergy dedicated to fostering the art of musical liturgy.

Printed in the United States of America

Acknowledgments

Excerpts from the English translation of *Rite of Marriage* © 1969, International Committee on English in the Liturgy, Inc. (ICEL); excerpts from the English translation of *The Roman Missal* © 1973, ICEL. All rights reserved.

Excerpts from the *Lectionary for Mass* © 1970 and *New American Bible* © 1970 by the Confraternity of Christian Doctrine, Washington, DC are used by license of copyright holder. All rights reserved.

Second Printing: Febuary, 1988
Third Printing: April, 1989
Fourth Printing: September, 1989

TABLE OF CONTENTS

PREFACE

As my own wedding day drew closer, two lists seemed to grow longer with each passing day: the list of things to do before the wedding, and the list of people to whom my wife and I owed a great deal of gratitude. The list of people who provided insight and support during the writing of this book seemed to grow as quickly.

Numerous colleagues in pastoral ministry offered suggestions and provided a wealth of practical, and oftentimes humorous, reflections on their experiences with weddings. I want to especially thank Laura Meagher, Jim Mongelluzzo, Deno and Monica Reed, and the members of the Marriage Preparation Teams at Holy Trinity Church in Washington, D.C.

Special thanks go to Georgetown University, Holy Trinity Church and the various individuals and foundations which sponsor The Georgetown Center for Liturgy, Spirituality and the Arts, and, thus, provided the time and resources for writing this book.

The Pastoral Press endorsed this venture in its infancy and continued to offer patient and encouraging support. My thanks to Dan Connors, Larry Johnson, Virgil Funk and Mary Ellen Cohn.

Larry Madden, Elaine Rendler and John Buscemi were much more than the authors of their respective chapters. They influenced this entire book, just as they have each been true friends and mentors in the art of pastoral liturgy.

Finally, I thank and dedicate this book to my wife, Anne, and my two sons, Matthew and Peter. Their love and encouragement made it all possible.

Paul Covino

INTRODUCTION

If you are like most engaged couples, you may have discovered by now that the joy, excitement and anticipation that accompanied the announcement of your engagement can quickly give way to anxiety, worry and tension as you prepare for the "big day." You may not have had any idea that getting married required a crash-course in musician's union regulations, the secrets of reserving a banquet hall within 30 miles of the church, and Emily Post's principles of excruciatingly correct wedding etiquette!

This small book has been designed to assist you with something that may have seemed equally veiled in mystery: the preparation of your wedding liturgy. Perhaps you were surprised to learn that you even had a role in this process. Years ago, the bride and groom had very little to say about their wedding liturgy because there was only one way to celebrate a wedding in the Roman Catholic Church. Following the Second Vatican Council, however, a revised *Rite of Marriage* was issued which allows several options in the wedding liturgy. This new rite clearly states that the couple is the minister of the sacrament of marriage and should be actively involved in the preparation of the wedding liturgy.

You are not alone in this undertaking. First of all, the priest or deacon who will preside at your wedding liturgy will work with you. Some parishes also have a liturgy coordinator, a wedding preparation committee, or a marriage preparation team to assist you. Undoubtedly, the parish music minister will be involved. Your parish can give you the names of the people available to help you.

This book is best used as a workbook; feel free to make notes throughout the book, as well as on the planning sheet toward the back. Chapter One provides background information and basic advice, while Chapters Two to Five give the actual texts for the wedding liturgy and information concerning music and environment. You should also be aware that many parishes and dioceses have specific guidelines relating to the wedding liturgy. Ask the priest or deacon working with you about any such guidelines early in the process.

Preparing your wedding liturgy is not difficult; it simply takes time and attention. What is true for shower parties, rehearsal dinners and the wedding reception is equally true for the wedding liturgy: if the basic elements have been prepared well ahead of time, everyone will be less anxious and really free to celebrate. From experience with hundreds of weddings, the four writers of this book can attest to the fact that the results will be well worth the effort.

Last but not least, preparing your wedding liturgy should be *fun*. You may have heard in marriage preparation sessions that communication is vitally important to a healthy marriage; let this preparation process be an opportunity to practice that skill. Discuss the various options in the liturgy with each other, pray over the scripture readings, be sensitive to one another's tastes, and be open to new ways of doing things. With this in mind, preparing your wedding liturgy can bring you closer together, and the result will be a liturgy that is festive and memorable for all involved.

CHAPTER ONE

AGE OLD TRADITIONS
AND TIMELY ADVICE

W hile finalizing plans with the bride for flowers in the church, the florist remarks, "It is customary, you know, to have a white runner rolled down the middle aisle before you enter. It's only plastic, but it is a traditional sign of honor." Uncertain but still smiling, the bride writes another check for fifty dollars.

Noticing the groom's five year old cousin wandering curiously around the tuxedo-clad mannequins, the salesman asks, "Is this young lad the ring-bearer? You know, the ringbearer's tux is free with the rental of six or more tuxedos. You are having a ring-bearer, aren't you?" Not wanting to hurt his young cousin's feelings, the groom agrees.

VENERABLE TRADITIONS

"Every tradition grows ever more venerable — the more remote is its origin, the more confused that origin is" (Friedrich Nietzsche, *Human All Too Human*, 1878).

• The custom of having the bridesmaids dress like the bride and the groomsmen like the groom was a way of protecting the bride and groom from evil spirits. If all the women were dressed similarly and all the men were dressed similarly, the evil spirits would not know who the real bride and groom were, and, thus, could not bother the couple.

• The custom whereby the groom is not permitted to see the bride before the wedding dates from a time when most marriages were arranged by the groom and the bride's father. In return for his daughter, the father received money or some other commodity from the groom. Often, the groom did not even meet his bride until the wedding when he made payment to the father. If the groom did not like what he saw, he could call off the wedding, and the father would not receive his payment. To avoid the possibility of such "bad luck," the father did not permit the groom to see the bride until the time of the transaction.

"The Sullivans had the most beautiful soloist for the *Ave Maria* at Sally's wedding last month, dear," mother says to daughter. "Who's going to sing it at your wedding?" "Bill and I hadn't planned on having the *Ave Maria*, mom," the daughter gingerly responds. Seeing the shock on her mother's face, the bride begrudgingly calls Mrs. Sullivan for the name of the soloist.

Do any of these scenes seem faintly familiar to you? Have you recently discovered, much to your surprise, that several of your relatives and friends are experts on every aspect of a wedding? Have you noticed an increase in the number of times you hear the phrases, "Naturally, you'll want to . . . ," "Of course, you must . . . ," "It is tradition that . . . ," "Etiquette would suggest . . . ," or "We've always done it this way . . . ?" Or are you learning more about the neighbor's daughter's wedding than you ever cared to know? If your answer to any of the above questions is "yes," be assured that you are not alone!

Many of the dos and don'ts one hears about weddings claim to be based on long-standing tradition. There is a popular assumption that weddings have always been celebrated in a certain way, and that certain practices are essential for a wedding to be considered "traditional." If these practices are not observed, the wedding is considered "untraditional" or "contemporary." Soon after announcing their engagement, many couples find themselves pressured into opting for one of these two styles.

The truth is that there has been quite an evolution in the understanding of marriage and in the way in which weddings have been celebrated. The history of marriage in the Roman Catholic Church spans almost two thousand years. It is a rich and diverse heritage, and one that will soon be further enriched by your wedding. Here are just a few highlights to indicate how the current wedding liturgy and some wedding customs developed:

- For one thousand years, there was no specifically Christian rite of marriage. Christians contracted marriage according to the civil and family ceremonies of their culture. Marriage was understood primarily as a contract between two families, usually arranged by the groom and the bride's father. As part of the contract, the bride left her family and joined the groom's family. This was expressed ritually by a procession in which the bride was escorted by her father to the groom's home where the father "gave the bride away" to the groom. Using the vows and symbols of their particular culture, the bride promised to be a good wife and mother, and the groom was recognized as the head of this new household.

- In the fourth century, some local churches developed simple marriage blessings for Christian couples, although there was still no church rite of marriage. After the wedding ceremony, the bishop or priest would visit the couple to congratulate them. The couple, in turn, would ask for his blessing on their marriage. As time passed, parts of the actual wedding ceremony came to be celebrated in the presence of a priest and, eventually, in the church building, constituting the core of the church's rite of marriage.

- In the early Middle Ages, civil government in much of western Europe was in a state of disarray following a period of political turmoil. In many areas, record keeping and other civic responsibilities fell to the strongest organization remaining in society, the church, whose clergy and monks were the largest educated group at the time. Thus, church officials began to exercise jurisdiction over certain aspects of marriage. By the eleventh century, most marriages were fully under church jurisdiction and were presided over by a priest.

DOWRIES

In ancient times, most marriages were arranged very much like a business deal. Services, property and even people were exchanged in order to gain a marriage partner. Usually, it was the bride who was "purchased" for her value as a household worker and childbearer. The bride's father expected something in return for the loss of his daughter.

In the centuries prior to the birth of Christ, this practice changed in some cultures. While the groom continued to give a gift to the bride's father, he also received goods, land or money along with the bride. This was the bride's *dowry*, supplied by her father to make her more attractive for marriage.

(For more information on dowries and other wedding customs, see *The Wedding Book* by Howard Kirshcenbaum and Rockwell Stensrud, Seabury Press, 1974.)

• Prior to the eleventh century, couples were permitted to exchange their marriage vows either in private or in a public ceremony. Since it happened that private marriages were occasionally used to force the bride into marriage without her consent, the church prohibited private marriages in the year 1215. In that same century, the church officially identified marriage as a sacrament. These two actions were reaffirmed at the Council of Trent in 1563 where a requirement that Catholics must marry in the presence of a priest and two or three witnesses was added.

• The wedding ceremony changed very little in the four centuries following the Council of Trent. Attitudes toward marriage did change, however, especially in the late nineteenth and twentieth centuries. The personal love between a man and a woman came to be recognized as the primary motivation for marriage, replacing contractual arrangements between families. The roles and societal expectations concerning men and women also began to change. The image of the husband as head of the household and the wife as obedient homemaker gave way to a view of the couple as two partners, each possessing talents and rights to a career, yet equally responsible for and involved in creating a home and family.

• In 1963, the church began a major reform of all the sacraments at the Second Vatican Council (1962-1965). The understanding, or theology, of marriage was redefined in light of the contemporary Christian experience of marriage. To reflect this new understanding, a revised wedding liturgy, the *Rite of Marriage*, was issued in 1969 and serves as the basis for all weddings in the Roman Catholic Church today, including the marriage of a Catholic and a non-Catholic.

In popular usage, the word "tradition" implies "no change." The surprising lesson from the history of Christian weddings is that change itself is part of the tradition. That is, marriage rites have changed at various times throughout history as the Christian understanding of marriage has developed. What makes the wedding liturgy traditional, then, is not simply the continued use of certain old or popular customs.

Similarly, "contemporary" and "untraditional" are labels often associated with weddings that do not follow an expected pattern or that have elements created by the couples themselves, such as the marriage vows. While the wedding liturgy does allow for a variety of options, it also has a given structure and provides formulas for the vows and other texts. Its celebration is governed by the liturgical guidelines of the church. A wedding is contemporary, therefore, not because of its originality or rejection of established patterns.

"Traditional" and "contemporary," as used in popular language, simply imply a particular style. When describing Church liturgies, however, they refer not to distinct styles, but to two inseparable characteristics that are always present. Your wedding liturgy will be traditional because it is based on the *Rite of Marriage* and, therefore, is faithful to the church's understanding of marriage. It will be contemporary because, as it is celebrated, the wedding liturgy will reveal your love for one another and make present here and now God's love for you in its actions and symbols. In other words, the wedding liturgy is both traditional and contemporary by its very nature.

So, what does this say about the task you are now facing — the preparation of your wedding liturgy? It says what this task is **not**:

Preparing the wedding liturgy is not a matter of creating a ceremony according to a particular style.

This does not mean that your wedding will not have a style of its own. It just means that style is not the primary consideration in preparing the wedding liturgy. There are more basic things to consider first.

This simple point may well be the most challenging one for couples today. Why? To put it bluntly, weddings are big business. From florists to professional wedding consultants, there is substantial pressure on couples to "go all out" in setting a style for the wedding. By now, you have probably discovered how expensive that can be. At the same time, you may be discovering that the more important and substantial aspects of the wedding can easily get overlooked in the rush to have everything "just so."

It doesn't have to be that way with your preparations for the wedding liturgy. Let this rule guide you and serve as a general job description:

The goal of your preparation is to encourage the full and active participation of all who will gather to celebrate your marriage. This is best accomplished by carefully preparing and celebrating the central features of the wedding liturgy. The primary focus of your attention, then, is the *Rite of Marriage,* in which the structure and individual elements of the wedding liturgy are presented. These are basic and essential to the wedding liturgy.

Nothing is more vital to effective liturgy than the active participation of all the worshippers. This was a basic premise of the Second Vatican Council. In the same way, the active participation, or lack of participation, of those who gather to celebrate your marriage will determine the quality of the wedding liturgy. It *is* possible to draw everyone — Catholics and non-Catholics, churchgoers and non-churchgoers — into the celebration of your marriage. It just requires some attention to the basic elements of the wedding liturgy. This is not difficult, but it will demand more of you than simple stylistic considerations.

The remainder of the book will discuss the basic elements of the wedding liturgy. As an introduction to that, here is some general advice to make your preparation as effective as possible.

ONE: Distinguish between what is essential and what is not.

As you review the wedding liturgy in Chapter Two, you may note that some of the practices that you may be accustomed to seeing at weddings are not listed. These are instances of popular practices which, although commonly used at weddings, are not actually part of the wedding liturgy. They fall into three categories: social customs, expressions of personal taste, and religious devotions. Each of these can enhance a wedding liturgy. It's all a matter of distinguishing them from what is essential and keeping them in perspective.

Social Customs. Couples often experience a great deal of pressure to shape their wedding according to others' expectations. This pressure is usually strongest when social customs are involved. These customs are not necessarily religious, nor do they necessarily reflect contemporary attitudes toward marriage. They are simply "expected social behavior."

Wearing special gowns and tuxedos, and having bridesmaids, flower girls, ringbearers and white aisle runners are all examples of social customs. So is the practice whereby the bride is "given away" by her father, and the practice of seating the relatives and friends of the groom on one side of the aisle and those of the bride on the other side. Some social customs are actually based in superstition, such

A WEDDING IS PUBLIC BUSINESS

The following is from an essay that appeared in TIME magazine in 1983:

The vows that couples devise are, with some exceptions, never as moving to the guests as they are to the couple. Too often the phrases, words over-blown and intimate and yearning all at once, go floating plumply around the altar, pink dreams of the ineffable. Friends and family lean forward in their pews. The clergy-person beams inscrutably, abetting the thing, but keeping counsel. The guests are both fascinated and faintly appalled to be privy to such intense and theatrical whisperings. John Lennon and Yoko Ono once held press conferences while lying in bed, and the effect of the self-made vows is sometimes obscurely the same... If the bride and groom have intimacies to whisper, there are private places for that. A wedding is public business.[1]

Contrary to popular opinion, "public" is not necessarily the opposite of "personal," and "personal" is not necessarily the same as "private." When the author of the essay portrayed the wedding as "public business," he was not denying its personal nature. He was stating that it is not a private affair. Twenty years

continued

as the practice whereby the groom is not allowed to see the bride before the wedding.

Expressions of Personal Taste. Your wedding is obviously a deeply personal event, and it is natural to want to personalize the wedding liturgy. The *Rite of Marriage* allows for this by providing many options. You may select, for example, the prayers and scripture readings from a number of possibilities. You will work with the parish musician on the selection of music for the wedding. You may be involved in selecting flowers and other elements for the environment inside the church. All of these will reflect your personal taste and your values.

There are other expressions of personal taste that go beyond the options provided in the wedding liturgy. For example, you may have a special song or perhaps a poem or story that reflects your love for one another. Because of their importance in your relationship, you may want to share them with the relatives and friends at your wedding. The meaning that they hold for you, however, will be very difficult to convey to others, especially within the brief time of the wedding liturgy when so much else is happening. Such elements might be more appropriate within some other part of the wedding celebration, such as the reception or rehearsal dinner.

Religious Devotions. The wedding liturgy is rich in religious symbolism, and the various readings and prayers provide a broad perspective on the Christian experience of marriage. As you review the options in Chapters Two to Five, your own religious faith will influence and be reflected in the choices you make.

As a further expression of their religious faith, some couples include in the ceremony religious devotions that are not actually part of the wedding liturgy. At some weddings, the bride places flowers before a statue of Mary.

Another example is the lighting of a "unity" or "marriage" candle from two smaller candles, representing the union of the bride and groom. These practices can be meaningful if they actually reflect an important element of the couple's faith. As with expressions of personal taste, the question to ask here is whether this personal meaning can be conveyed effectively to others within the wedding liturgy. Perhaps such devotions could add a healthy religious dimension to other parts of the celebration, such as the reception or rehearsal dinner.

TWO: Give priority in your preparation and in the celebration to the essentials.

Let's take a look at what is already in place in the liturgy before your preparations even begin: a gathering of people, two processions, two or three scripture readings, a homily, general intercessions, the blessing and exchange of rings, the vows and a variety of related prayers. When the wedding takes place within Mass, all the regular elements of a Sunday eucharist are also involved. Usually, a fair amount of music is included. In other words, quite a bit takes place within a single liturgy, usually lasting no more than an hour.

In liturgy, it is more effective to do a few things well than to try to do many things. Quality is more important than quantity. Put your energy, then, into the essentials, that is, into reviewing and making the most of the options already contained in the *Rite of Marriage*. Avoid the temptation to add anything to the liturgy until you've exhausted all the possibilities in the rite.

Finally, ask the following questions of any practices that you consider adding to the wedding liturgy: Does it add something that is not already in the liturgy? Does it reflect a Christian understanding of marriage? Does it reflect your personal faith and values, or is it simply

A Wedding is Public Business *continued*

before this essay appeared, the Second Vatican Council presented a similar sentiment: "Liturgical services pertain to the whole Body of the Church."[2]

To say that "a wedding is public business" is not only to acknowledge the presence of others in the church; it implies preparing the wedding in such a way as to encourage their active participation in it. This principle is a helpful guide to determine whether some social custom, expression of personal taste or religious devotion that you are considering adding to the wedding liturgy will be effective.

(1) "The Hazards of Homemade Vows" by Lance Morrow, TIME, June 27, 1983, p. 78.

(2) *Constitution on the Sacred Liturgy*, no. 26. More on this quote in "Your Wedding: A Celebration for the Whole Church" in Chapter Two.

something you saw done at a friend's wedding? Does it encourage the participation of those who will gather to celebrate your marriage, or does it render them merely spectators? In summary, will it help to highlight, rather than obscure, the basic elements of the wedding liturgy?

THREE: Plan the wedding day as a whole, with the liturgy as its centerpiece.

At some weddings, the events that come before and after the liturgy are fun and full of human warmth, while the liturgy itself is stilted, cold and out of character with the rest of the day. People breathe a sigh of relief when the socially enforced rigidity of the ceremony is over and they can move on to the "real celebration" — the reception.

Yes, the wedding liturgy is a different kind of event than the reception; it has a form and spirit that are unique. When prepared and celebrated well, though, the wedding liturgy can be the high point of the day, an event of even more human warmth than the reception. The essential ingredient to make this happen is hospitality, the deliberate and conscious effort to welcome and pay attention to the people who will gather to celebrate your marriage.

FOUR: Do not underestimate the power of the non-verbal elements of the wedding liturgy.

The wedding liturgy is more than a series of prayers, readings and verbal commentary. It is a ritual act made up of significant symbols, gestures and texts. The music, the environment of the church building, the manner in which people are greeted, the way that processions move, the program or worship aid given to people for the liturgy, the placement of the couple and other worshippers: all of these will "speak" as loudly as will the prayers, readings, and other texts of the liturgy. When carefully prepared, these non-verbal elements complement the verbal ones; ignored or poorly prepared and celebrated, they can negate even the most beautiful of texts.

FIVE: Take advantage of the people who will be preparing the wedding liturgy with you.

In the introduction, we said that you are not alone in the preparation of the wedding liturgy. This is both reassurance and advice: reassurance that others will work with you, and advice to take advantage of them.

First of all, both the bride and the groom are involved in the preparation. This is not "her special day" any more than it is "his special day." It is a special day for the couple and the church. This is evident in the *Rite of Marriage* which consistently emphasizes the unity of the bride and groom in all aspects of the wedding.

Others who will work with you are the priest or deacon who will preside at the liturgy and the parish music minister. If your parish has a liturgy coordinator, wedding preparation committee or marriage preparation team, they may also be involved. These people have been chosen by your parish to assist you. They bring a great deal of experience to the job. Share your ideas with them, and be open to their advice.

SIX: Don't wait until the last minute to prepare the wedding liturgy!

Can you imagine planning the wedding reception on one week's notice? In the same way, give yourselves — and others — plenty of time to prepare the wedding liturgy. Talk, discuss, review the options, make the necessary arrangements well in advance. The wedding rehearsal is just what the name implies: a rehearsal of what has already been decided. It is not the time to make decisions about liturgical options. If the preparations have been done well in advance, there is no reason why the rehearsal needs to be any longer than thirty minutes. Let the priest, deacon or liturgy coordinator run the rehearsal. Get through the rehearsal efficiently, and then go enjoy the company of family and friends!

The next four chapters will present the four major areas for your consideration: the wedding liturgy, the readings, the music, and the environment. A work sheet is provided at the back of the book for you to indicate your planning decisions as you go through these chapters.

CHAPTER TWO

THE CEREMONY: THE WEDDING LITURGY

O nce you have decided to celebrate your marriage in the Roman Catholic Church, the first step is to contact your parish. This should not be delayed since many parishes now require a minimum of several months between this initial contact with the parish and the wedding date. During these months, you will probably be asked to participate in a parish or diocesan marriage preparation process. This is also the time to begin the preparations for your wedding liturgy.

The first two issues in your wedding liturgy preparations are very basic: the place and the date.

YOUR WEDDING: A CELEBRATION FOR THE WHOLE CHURCH

Liturgical services are not private functions but are celebrations of the Church which is "the sacrament of unity" ... Liturgical services pertain to the whole Body of the Church. They manifest it, and have effects upon it. But they also touch individual members of the Church in different ways, depending on their orders, their role in the liturgical services, and their actual participation in them ... Rites which are meant to be celebrated in common, with the faithful present and actively participating, should as far as possible be celebrated in that way rather than by an individual and quasi-privately.[1]

This statement from the Second Vatican Council presents one of the most basic characteristics of Christian liturgy: its communal nature. All liturgy takes place in the context of a particular parish community within the context of the universal church.

While the wedding liturgy will touch you, your family and friends in an especially intimate way, it pertains to the local parish and to the larger church as well. When you exchange your vows, you offer a visible sign of God's presence and love to the

continued

PLACE

When marriage was viewed as primarily a family affair, the family home was the appropriate and ordinary place for the wedding celebration. As the marriage of Christians came to be seen in the larger context of the church, the ordinary place for the wedding celebration became the parish church. This remains true today. (See "Your Wedding: A Celebration for the Whole Church," left.)

The wedding liturgy is celebrated in the parish church of the bride or the groom. There is no longer a preference for the bride's parish over the groom's parish. The important thing is to celebrate your wedding in the parish where one or both of you are members. Often, it is required that you be registered as parishioners before the wedding can be scheduled. This is a formal acknowledgment that you are members of the parish in which the wedding will be celebrated.

DATE AND TIME

In general, a wedding liturgy may be celebrated on any day of the year. There are various considerations, though, that make certain days and times more appropriate than others.

(1) **The parish schedule.** Parishes often have a fixed schedule of times for weddings based on the availability of the church, the priests or deacons, and the musicians. Other parish activities may also restrict certain dates and times. For example, Sunday weddings are not possible in some parishes because of the regular Mass schedule. Ask the priest or deacon about your parish schedule.

(2) **Special seasons.** Lent is a season of penance in preparation for Easter, while Advent looks ahead to Christmas and to Christ's second coming at the end of time. The tone of the church's worship during these times is more

subdued. This may be reflected quite visibly in the church environment during Advent and Lent (see Chapter Five). While weddings are not prohibited during these times, other times of the year are more appropriate for the festive nature of the wedding liturgy. (The dates for Advent and Lent vary from year to year, so check with your parish for this year's dates.)

There is one last piece of advice concerning the date and time of your wedding. It is very practical and can save you a lot of unnecessary trouble:

Make sure you have reserved the date and time of your wedding with the parish before printing the invitations or reserving the reception facilities.

THE PEOPLE IN YOUR WEDDING LITURGY

Next, we turn our attention to the people who will play a part in your wedding liturgy celebration. As you know from Sunday Mass, there are a variety of roles within the liturgy. These various roles are defined as "ministries," and the people who fulfill them as "ministers."

The Assembly

As at any liturgy, the fundamental ministry within the wedding liturgy is that of the assembly of people who gather to celebrate and witness your marriage. Everyone in the church for your wedding is, first and foremost, a member of this assembly — the two of you, the wedding party, the priest or deacon, and the musicians included. The assembly celebrates the liturgy; individual members of this assembly fulfill various special ministries within the liturgy.

You may have been to weddings where this point was more or less overlooked, with the result that the majority of people at the wed-

parish in which your wedding is celebrated. You create a new family within that community. At the same time, the church and, in particular, the local parish promise to be there for you in times of joy and in times of need. You are making a commitment to each other and to the church. In turn, the church is making a commitment to you.

The guidelines which many parishes and dioceses have established for weddings reflect this commitment. The church's concern is expressed before the wedding in its encouragement to you to take part in a marriage preparation process. This concern continues in the assistance and guidance which the parish offers for your wedding liturgy. As a liturgy of the parish, your wedding will be influenced and shaped by the parish's regular patterns of worship, especially its celebration of Sunday Mass. Look upon these guidelines not as obstacles to be overcome, but rather as an expression of the church's desire to celebrate your wedding as an integral and welcome part of the parish's worship life.

(1) *Constitution on the Sacred Liturgy,* nos. 26-27.

ding were treated like an audience at a show. When this happens, people refrain from participating in the liturgy, and the whole experience can end up being about as engaging as watching someone else's home movies! Recall our general job description from Chapter One:

The goal of your preparation is to encourage the full and active participation of all who will gather to celebrate your marriage.

Since the wedding liturgy is a parish celebration, it is preferable that parishioners, as well as family and friends from outside the parish, be part of the assembly. To encourage this, some parishes announce weddings in the parish bulletin with an invitation for parishioners to participate in the liturgy. In other places, weddings are occasionally celebrated within regularly scheduled Sunday and Saturday evening Masses so that the community may be present.

The Couple

The two of you are the ministers of the sacrament of marriage in the Roman Catholic wedding liturgy. You give yourselves to one another in marriage. The priest or deacon serves as the church's official witness, but he does not "pronounce you man and wife."

Since a great deal of attention is focused on you during the wedding, you also set the tone for the assembly by your own attitudes and behavior. If, for example, you are at ease before the liturgy and taking the time to greet people as they arrive, people will feel welcome and relaxed. If you enter into the prayers and singing during the liturgy, others in the assembly will be inclined to follow your lead.

Although permitted, it is not recommended that you take on additional ministries during the liturgy, such as reader or communion minister. These other ministries are best fulfilled by others in the assembly. The roles mentioned in the previous two paragraphs will require most of your energy and attention if they are to be done well.

The Presider

In most cases, a priest will preside, or officiate, at the wedding liturgy. When the wedding is celebrated without Mass, a deacon may preside. In either case, a priest or deacon from the parish usually fulfills this role since the wedding is seen as a parish celebration. Priests or deacons from outside the parish may preside at weddings with the permission of the local pastor. If the priest or deacon is from out of state, he must also obtain a civil license from the state in which the wedding will take place to officiate at the wedding.

The presence of "concelebrants," or priests other than the presider in the sanctuary, is permitted but not highly recommended since it visibly detracts from the central role of the couple as minister of the sacrament. Priests need not assist as "concelebrants" in order to participate in your wedding. They can sit with the other members of the assembly in the church, and can, instead, be asked to lead a blessing at the reception, rehearsal dinner or some other part of the wedding festivities.

As marriages between Catholics and non-Catholics become increasingly common, it is not unusual for the couple to invite a minister from the non-Catholic parish to be involved in the wedding liturgy. This minister may, for example, lead one of the prayers or blessings. Certain parts of the wedding liturgy, such as the questions concerning the consent and exchange of vows, are reserved to the Catholic priest or deacon, however. Speak with the priest or deacon before extending an invitation to another minister, and discuss the logistics of who will do and say what well in advance of

WHEN A CATHOLIC MARRIES A NON-CATHOLIC

Years ago, it was not unusual for a non-Catholic engaged to a Catholic to "convert" to Catholicism prior to the wedding. Often, this was done to avoid any conflict that a difference of religions may have presented to the marriage and to the upbringing of children.

Today, the situation is somewhat different. While the number of marriages between Catholics and non-Catholics has increased over the last twenty years, more and more of these couples have decided to maintain their different religious affiliations. The Catholic Church's own policy for receiving new members (The Rite of Christian Initiation of Adults and the Reception into Full Communion with the Catholic Church) is sensitive to this concern and cautions against joining the church only because of an upcoming marriage to a Catholic.

When a Catholic marries a non-Catholic, the church's concern is that the Catholic be able to remain active in his or her faith and that, as far as possible, any children be brought up as Catholics. The priest or deacon writes to the local bishop to apply for one of the following:

Permission to Enter into a Mixed Marriage: for a Catholic

continued

the rehearsal. If planned and carried out well, this can be a beautiful and significant sign of the ecumenical dimension of your marriage. (See "When a Catholic Marries a Non-Catholic," left.)

The Witnesses

Every member of the assembly at your wedding is a witness to your exchange of vows. At the same time, three particular witnesses have a special role to play in the liturgy and for church records. First, the church's "official witness" is the priest or deacon who asks for and receives your consent. He does this by asking you the three questions in the statement of intentions and by receiving your consent in the exchange of vows. The other two witnesses stand by you during the marriage rite. They need not be Catholic or even baptized; their primary duty is to attest to the fact that the marriage took place. While it is customary to have one male ("the best man") and one female ("the maid of honor"), it is possible to have two males or two females.

Ushers

The stereotyped image of the usher at a wedding is the groom's college buddy or business associate, dressed in a tuxedo with a tie that's too tight around the neck, and somewhat fatigued after being out most of the previous night at the bachelor party. He meets people at the door of the church with outstretched elbow, looking as stiff as a well-starched shirt.

To be most helpful at your wedding, the usher should be a very different character. More and more, this role is being referred to as "the ministry of hospitality." While it may sound foreign, this title gives a better indication of the usher's principal duties: to cordially greet people arriving at the church, give them a program or order of service, and assist them in finding a seat near other worshippers. Men and women may serve as ushers; there is no reason to limit the role to men.

The Musicians

The number and type of musicians involved in your wedding liturgy will depend on the specific musical program that you work out with the parish music minister. The various possibilities are discussed in detail in Chapter Four. Since music plays such an important role in the liturgy, one particular recommendation will be made here.

The music at your wedding has the power to encourage or stifle the participation of the assembly. The norm in the Roman Catholic liturgy is participatory music; that is, the majority of music during the liturgy should be sung by the entire assembly. A cantor, or leader of song, can significantly enhance the assembly's participation in the liturgy by reviewing music that may be unfamiliar before the liturgy and by providing subtle direction during the liturgy. The spirit and enthusiasm that the assembly's participation in the singing will bring to your wedding liturgy will be well worth the relatively small expense of hiring a leader of song.

Readers

In some places, parishioners who read regularly at Sunday Mass fulfill this role at weddings. The advantage to this is that such people are accustomed to reading in that particular church and know the logistics of such things as the microphones. If this is not the practice in your parish, you will want to select readers from among the people who will be at the wedding. People who serve as readers in their home parishes are good choices because of their familiarity with the role. Otherwise, look for people who are good public speakers. More on this in Chapter Three.

marrying someone who is baptized but is not a Catholic.

Dispensation from Disparity of Cult: for a Catholic marrying someone who is not baptized.

These are required whenever a Catholic marries a non-Catholic, whether the wedding is celebrated in a Catholic church or in another place.

An additional request is involved if the wedding itself is going to be celebrated outside of a Catholic church:

Dispensation from Canonical Form: required when someone other than a Catholic priest or deacon is going to receive the consent (or vows). Usually, this means that the wedding is going to be celebrated in a non-Catholic church, and the minister from the non-Catholic parish will preside.

Permission to Celebrate the Wedding Outside of a Church: required, as the title indicates, when the wedding is going to be celebrated in a place other than a church. This permission is often sought when a Catholic marries a Jew, Muslim or other non-Christian.

Communion Ministers
(Weddings within Mass only)

In order to facilitate the distribution of communion, especially if under the forms of both bread and wine, communion ministers should be selected to assist the priest. As with readers, communion ministers from the parish are ideal since they are familiar with the procedures. Otherwise, think of people who will be at your wedding who are communion ministers in their home parishes. Finally, with the permission of the parish priest, members of the assembly who are not commissioned as communion ministers may be asked to serve in this role for this special event.

Altar Servers

Altar servers, or "altar boys," assist the presider in a number of ways during the liturgy. Some parishes automatically schedule them for weddings; others do not use them for weddings. Check with the parish priest about the local practice, or if you wish to ask a relative or friend who is an altar server at another parish to serve at your wedding. In this case, it would also be wise to ask the altar server(s) to attend the rehearsal. If a person has never been an altar server, it would not be appropriate to ask him to serve in this role at the wedding liturgy.

PHOTOGRAPHS AND VIDEOTAPES

Photographs and videotapes serve as an attractive reminder of your wedding, but you don't want the taking of pictures to interfere with the event itself. Through the use of various lenses and film speeds, a professional photographer need not be right up front in order to get good pictures. He or she can be positioned discreetly to the side and back of the church. Ask the photographer in advance to keep his or her movements around the church to a minimum during the liturgy. Most parishes also allow a period of time before or after the liturgy for formal posing of pictures.

A bigger challenge might be to keep the amateur photographers among your family and friends under control during the liturgy. People standing up to take pictures not only distract from what is going on, but they also block the vision of those seated behind them. Perhaps a politely worded note could be included in the program asking people to refrain from snapping pictures until after the liturgy.

PROGRAMS

A well designed printed program, or order of service, can greatly enhance the assembly's participation in the liturgy. It should include the music that the assembly will be asked to sing, as well as an outline of the liturgy and subtle directions as to when to sit or stand for those who may be unfamiliar with the Roman Catholic wedding liturgy. The texts of the vows, the readings and the prayers spoken by the priest or deacon should not be printed. The assembly participates by listening to these parts of the liturgy, not by reading them. Three sample programs are provided in the back of this book. Your parish may also have a format for a program.

The parish music minister can provide you with the music and words of the songs for the program. He or she can also help you to arrange the necessary permission to reprint the music in your program. Reprinting music, even just the words of a song, without the permission of the publisher is a violation of United States Copyright Law. The benefit of having the music easily accessible to the assembly will be well worth the few phone calls or letters required to obtain reprint permission.

THREE FORMS OF THE WEDDING LITURGY

The *Rite of Marriage* provides three forms for celebrating marriage in the Roman Catholic Church:

I. **The Rite for Celebrating Marriage During Mass** is normally used when two Catholics marry.

II. **The Rite for Celebrating Marriage Outside Mass** is used when a Catholic marries a baptized person from another Christian Church.

III. **The Rite for Celebrating Marriage Between a Catholic and an Unbaptized Person** is used when a Catholic marries someone who is not Christian.

In the first form, the wedding is situated in the context of a Mass. In the second and third forms, Mass is not celebrated. Each of the forms is equally valid in the eyes of the Church; a wedding is not any more or less complete because of the celebration of Mass.

There is some flexibility in which form may be used. For example, it is possible to use the rite for marriage within Mass when a Catholic marries a non-Catholic, but it is not encouraged since current church regulations essentially prohibit non-Catholics from receiving communion at Mass. In this case, the celebration of Mass may serve as a source of disunity at a time when you want to stress unity. There are also times when the rite for marriage outside Mass is more appropriate for a Catholic couple. The second form may be the more honest choice if, for example, you are both Catholics but do not participate in the Mass on a regular basis. The choice of which form you will use should be made in consultation with the priest or deacon.

The prayers and readings used in each of the three forms are, generally, the same. The three forms also have the same basic structure:

GATHERING AND ENTRANCE RITES
LITURGY OF THE WORD
LITURGY OF THE SACRAMENT
   (MARRIAGE/EUCHARIST)
CONCLUDING RITES

At a wedding Mass, the marriage rite (that is, the consent or exchange of vows, and the exchange of rings) takes place after the homily and before the liturgy of the eucharist. When the wedding takes place outside Mass, the marriage rite is followed by the concluding rites.

Here is the outline of each of the three forms:

I. RITE FOR CELEBRATING MARRIAGE DURING MASS

GATHERING AND ENTRANCE RITES

1. Gathering of the Assembly
2. Procession
3. Greeting
4. Penitential Rite
5. Gloria
6. Opening Prayer

LITURGY OF THE WORD

7. Old Testament Reading
8. Responsorial Psalm
9. New Testament Reading
10. Gospel Acclamation
11. Gospel
12. Homily

MARRIAGE RITE

13. Address and Statement of Intentions
14. Consent and Exchange of Vows
15. Blessing and Exchange of Rings
16. General Intercessions

BRINGING THE FORMS TO LIFE

Take a look at one of your cookbooks. (You must have received at least one at showers by now!) Do you see how recipes are usually set up? First, there's a list of the ingredients in the order they are mixed in. Then, there's a description of the actions (chop, fry, etc.) needed to bring these ingredients to life as a cake, pie or fettucine alfredo.

The outline of the three forms of marriage on these pages is similar to the list of ingredients in a recipe. It's simply a list of what happens when. To prepare the wedding liturgy effectively, it's also necessary to know what energies are needed to bring these elements to life.

Fr. Eugene Walsh, S. S. offers a concise summary of these energies. What he says about Sunday Mass is equally applicable to the wedding liturgy:

> The members of the assembly have three things to do at Sunday Mass. They must gather, they must listen, they must respond. Nobody else can do these actions. If the assembly does them deliberately and with energy, the Sunday Mass becomes life-giving. If the assembly does not do them, or does them poorly, the life-giving power of Sunday Mass is severely reduced.[1]

continued

LITURGY OF THE EUCHARIST

17. Preparation of the Gifts
18. Eucharistic Prayer
19. The Lord's Prayer
20. Nuptial Blessing
21. Sign of Peace
22. Breaking of the Bread
23. Communion
24. Prayer after Communion

CONCLUDING RITES

25. Blessing
26. Dismissal
27. Recessional

II. RITE FOR CELEBRATING MARRIAGE OUTSIDE MASS

GATHERING AND ENTRANCE RITES

1. Gathering of the Assembly
2. Procession
3. Greeting
4. Opening Prayer

LITURGY OF THE WORD

5. Old Testament Reading
6. Responsorial Psalm
7. New Testament Reading
8. Gospel Acclamation
9. Gospel
10. Homily

MARRIAGE RITE

11. Address and Statement of Intentions
12. Consent and Exchange of Vows
13. Blessing and Exchange of Rings
14. General Intercessions
15. Nuptial Blessing

CONCLUDING RITES

16. The Lord's Prayer
17. Blessing
18. Recessional

III. RITE FOR CELEBRATING MARRIAGE BETWEEN A CATHOLIC AND AN UNBAPTIZED PERSON

GATHERING AND ENTRANCE RITES

1. Gathering of the Assembly
2. Procession
3. Rite of Welcome

LITURGY OF THE WORD

4. Old Testament Reading
5. Responsorial Psalm
6. New Testament Reading
7. Gospel Acclamation
8. Gospel
9. Homily

MARRIAGE RITE

10. Address and Statement of Intentions
11. Consent and Exchange of Vows
12. Blessing and Exchange of Rings
13. General Intercessions
14. Nuptial Blessing

CONCLUDING RITES

15. The Lord's Prayer
16. Blessing
17. Recessional

Bringing the Forms to Life *continued*

The gathering and entrance rites of the liturgy are designed to transform the many individuals in the church into a unified assembly of worshippers, ready to celebrate and hear the scriptures.

During the liturgy of the word, the energy involved is listening, both to the scriptures and to the homily.

In the marriage rite, you respond to the scripture readings in your exchange of vows. The assembly responds as the witnesses to this sacrament, pledging their support to you. When marriage is celebrated within Mass, the energy of responding continues in the eucharistic prayer and in communion.

Finally, the response to God's word continues in daily life each time we attend to the needs of others. The two of you carry on this response each day of married life as your love develops and a new Christian family is established.

(1) *A Parish Program for Making a Life-Giving Church* (Pastoral Arts Associates of North America, 1985), Part III, p. 44.

STEP BY STEP THROUGH THE WEDDING LITURGY

Once you have identified which of the three forms of marriage you will be using, the next step is to review each of the individual elements of the liturgy. Note those places where there are options and discuss which option you prefer, indicating your choices on the planning sheet in the back of the book. The commentary which accompanies each section describes the purpose of that element of the liturgy, and suggests ways to make that element most effective.

Phrases in some of the prayers are in parentheses. These phrases may be omitted if appropriate. You will also see the letter "N" in a number of the prayers. This simply indicates where your names would be inserted in the prayer. Finally, occasional suggestions are given in the margin for alternative language that does not exclude women.

GATHERING AND ENTRANCE RITES

Gathering of the Assembly

Take a look at the list of people who will be at your wedding: relatives of the bride, relatives of the groom, friends and associates from work and school, people from different parts of the country or from other countries, Catholics from other parishes, Catholics who are not regular church-goers, non-Catholics and non-Christians who may be unfamiliar with the Catholic liturgy or even uncomfortable in a Catholic church. At the wedding, these various people — many of whom may not know one another — will come together to witness and celebrate your marriage.

People are generally more at ease and open to celebrate when they know the people around them. At weddings, this often does not happen until sometime during the reception. People come into the church as strangers and leave as strangers, so it's no wonder they are reticent in joining in the liturgy. Some very simple things can be done as people arrive at the church to make them feel welcome and to gather them into an assembly that is ready to celebrate the liturgy together. For this reason, the time before the entrance procession is one of the best opportunities to set a positive tone for the wedding. Consider the following ways to take advantage of this opportunity:

(a) "Get me to the church on time!" In fact, plan on arriving about one half hour before the time of the wedding. Give yourselves time to relax at the church and, in fairness to others, start the wedding on time.

(b) By all means, get dressed at home. Some parishes do provide room for changing, but fussing over gowns and tuxedos that soon before the wedding usually only adds to the anxiety and increases the blood pressure. For the sake of a few wrinkles, it's not worth it.

(c) Make sure that people are warmly greeted as they arrive at the church, preferably by the two of you and your parents. This is probably the single most effective thing you can do to make people feel welcome, to thank them for joining in this special celebration, and to encourage their participation in the liturgy. This also allows you to introduce friends and relatives *before* the liturgy, rather than waiting until the reception. Such interaction in church is not irreverent; it serves to shape a worshipping assembly out of the many individuals who will be at your wedding.

(Couples who have personally greeted people before the wedding liturgy have reported two added benefits to the practice: these introductions often take the place of the sometimes monotonous receiving line during the reception, and, since your attention is on greeting people before the wedding, you don't have time to worry about being nervous!)

(d) Avoid prelude music that is overpowering or somber. Pleasant, upbeat music in the church as people arrive contributes to effective gathering. (See Chapter Four for specific suggestions.)

(e) Seat people close together and toward the front of the church. While the first one or two pews are often reserved for the immediate family, the other front pews should be filled as people arrive. Fill one pew before seating people in the next. There is also no reason to have a "bride's side" and a "groom's side" in the church. The aim is to encourage people to interact and form a cohesive assembly, not to separate them into different contingents. Ushers, bridesmaids and other people can assist in seating people; this role is not limited to males.

(f) Just before the entrance procession, the leader of song could briefly rehearse music that might be unfamiliar as a way to encourage people to sing during the liturgy.

Procession

The entrance procession at a wedding is an extended form of the regular entrance of the priest and other ministers at Sunday Mass. The *Rite of Marriage* describes the procession in this way: " . . . the ministers go first, followed by the priest, and then the bride and bridegroom. According to local custom, they may be escorted by at least their parents and the two witnesses" (no. 20). Adaptations may be made to this format, such as the inclusion of ushers and bridesmaids in addition to the two witnesses ("best man" and "maid of honor") in the procession lineup. The procession may also be simplified so that the two of you enter alone in procession and meet the priest at the front of the aisle.

The *Rite of Marriage* does not mention the form of procession in which the bride enters, accompanied by the bridesmaids and her father, and meets the groom at the front of the aisle. This form developed at a time when a wedding literally signified the transfer of the bride between two men: from father to husband (see "Venerable Traditions" in Chapter One). Many couples — certainly many women — would not see their wedding in this light today! The procession, as envisioned in the *Rite of Marriage,* is the ritual entrance of the ministers for the liturgy. Since the two of you together are the ministers of the sacrament of marriage, you are both included in the procession.

A suggested order for the procession is the following: an usher carrying a processional cross, a reader carrying the Lectionary (the book of scripture readings for the liturgy), the priest or deacon, other ushers and bridesmaids, the groom escorted by his parents, and the bride escorted by her parents. If there are altar servers, they could walk in front of the priest or deacon. If a minister from another church is involved, he or she could walk next to or in front of the priest or deacon. The two of you could also walk in together at the end of the procession, with your parents in front of you. Once the procession has reached the front of the aisle, you could each kiss your parents. Then, all go to their respective places. (See Chapter Five for specific suggestions about seating arrangements for the couple, witnesses, ushers and bridesmaids.)

Greeting

Once everyone is in place and the music has ended, the presider formally begins the liturgy with the sign of the cross, the traditional beginning of Christian prayer:

Presider: **In the name of the Father, and of the Son, and of the Holy Spirit.**

All respond: **Amen.**

He then greets all present with one of the following greetings:

1. **The grace of our Lord Jesus Christ and the love of God and the fellowship of the Holy Spirit be with you all.**

2. **The grace and peace of God our Father and the Lord Jesus Christ be with you.**

3. **The Lord be with you.**

The response in each case is: **And also with you.** Although not mentioned in the *Rite of Marriage*, it would be appropriate for you, as ministers of the sacrament, to briefly greet people in your own words after the presider's greeting. If you plan to do this, ask the priest or deacon if a microphone could be placed near where you will be standing. After the greeting(s), a hymn could be sung by the entire assembly. Known as a "gathering song," this is an effective opportunity for the assembly to join their voices in prayer at the beginning of the liturgy. (See Chapter Four for suggestions.)

Penitential Rite
(Weddings within Mass only)

The penitential rite is the opportunity to recall our sinfulness and to ask the Lord's mercy. In keeping with the nature of the wedding liturgy, this rite is kept very simple. The priest begins with these or similar words: **My brothers and sisters, to prepare ourselves to celebrate the sacred mysteries, let us call to mind our sins.** Then, one of the following is used:

1. All say the following:
   I confess to almighty God,
   and to you, my brothers and sisters,
   that I have sinned through my own fault
   in my thoughts and in my words,
   in what I have done,
   and in what I have failed to do;
   and I ask blessed Mary, ever virgin,
   all the angels and saints,
   and you, my brothers and sisters,
   to pray for me to the Lord our God.

2. Priest: **Lord, we have sinned against you.**
   All: **Lord, have mercy.**

   Priest: **Lord, show us your mercy and love.**
   All: **And grant us your salvation.**

3. Priest: **You were sent to heal the contrite:**
   Lord, have mercy.
   All: **Lord, have mercy.**

   Priest: **You came to call sinners:**
   Christ, have mercy.
   All: **Christ, have mercy.**

   Priest: **You plead for us at the right hand**
   of the Father:
   Lord, have mercy.
   All: **Lord, have mercy.**

In each case, the priest then says:

   May almighty God have mercy on us,
   forgive us our sins,
   and bring us to everlasting life.

All respond: **Amen.** If option 1 or 2 was used, the following invocations conclude the penitential rite:

Priest: **Lord, have mercy.**
All: **Lord, have mercy.**

Priest: **Christ, have mercy.**
All: **Christ, have mercy.**

Priest: **Lord, have mercy.**
All: **Lord, have mercy.**

Gloria
(Weddings within Mass only)

If the wedding takes place on a Sunday outside of Advent or Lent or on a solemnity (that is, a major church feast day), the Gloria is the next prayer of the wedding liturgy. Otherwise, it is not used.

Glory to God in the highest,
and peace to his people on earth.
Lord God, heavenly King,
almighty God and Father,
we worship you, we give you thanks,
we praise you for your glory.
Lord Jesus Christ, only Son of the Father,
Lord God, Lamb of God,
you take away the sin of the world:
have mercy on us;
you are seated at the right hand of the Father:
receive our prayer.
For you alone are the Holy One,
you alone are the Lord,
you alone are the Most High,
Jesus Christ,
with the Holy Spirit,
in the glory of God the Father. Amen.

Opening Prayer

The presider than says **Let us pray**, pauses for a moment of silent prayer, and then says one of the following options for the opening prayer:

1. **Father,**
you have made the bond of marriage
a holy mystery,
a symbol of Christ's love for his Church.
Hear our prayers for N. and N.
With faith in you and in each other
they pledge their love today.

May their lives always bear witness
to the reality of that love.

We ask this through our Lord Jesus Christ,
   your Son,
who lives and reigns with you and the
   Holy Spirit,
one God, for ever and ever.

2. Father,
   hear our prayers for N. and N.,
   who today are united in marriage
      before your altar.
   Give them your blessing,
   and strengthen their love for each other.

   We ask this through our Lord Jesus Christ,
      your Son,
   who lives and reigns with you and the
      Holy Spirit,
   one God, for ever and ever.

3. Almighty God,
   hear our prayers for N. and N.,
   who have come here today
   to be united in the sacrament of marriage.
   Increase their faith in you and in each
      other,
   and through them bless your Church
   (with Christian children).

   We ask this through our Lord Jesus Christ,
      your Son,
   who lives and reigns with you and the
      Holy Spirit,
   one God, for ever and ever.

4. Father,
   when you created mankind
   you willed that man and wife should
      be one.
   Bind N. and N.
   in the loving union of marriage;
   and make their love fruitful
   so that they may be living witnesses
   to your divine love in the world.

Language note:
   "When you created humanity"
could be substituted for "when
you created mankind" in selection #4 for the opening prayer

my favorite

We ask this through our Lord Jesus Christ,
   your Son,
who lives and reigns with you and the
   Holy Spirit,
one God, for ever and ever.

The response in each case is: **Amen.**

LITURGY OF THE WORD

The focus of this section of the wedding liturgy is the proclamation of God's Word in the scripture readings. Since this is discussed in detail in other chapters, it will not be repeated here. Chapter Three provides the options for the Old Testament reading, the New Testament reading and the gospel, as well as commentary on each. The responsorial psalm and gospel acclamation are intended to be sung; they are discussed in Chapter Four.

The homily is delivered by a priest or deacon, normally the presider. It addresses the sacramental nature of Christian marriage as exemplified in the readings that have just been proclaimed and in your own lives. If the priest or deacon does not know you very well, he may try to find out more about you in your meetings with him before the wedding. In this way, he can prepare a homily that is personalized.

MARRIAGE RITE

The marriage rite is the central part of the wedding liturgy. Through the prayers and actions of this rite, you give yourselves to one another in marriage freely and unconditionally in the presence of the church's witnesses: the priest or deacon, the best man and maid of honor, and the entire assembly. Consider the following ways to enhance the power of this rite:

(a) Stand in such a way that you are both facing the assembly, with the best man and maid of honor standing to either side of you. The priest or deacon stands facing you, either directly in front of you or slightly to the side so that his back is not to the assembly. The assembly should remain seated so that all might be able to have a clear line of vision. (See Chapter Five for specific diagrams.)

(b) Have a microphone placed in front of you so that all might hear what is being said. This is, after all, the high point of the liturgy and all the witnesses — assembly included — should be able to hear it.

(c) Allow the prayers and symbolic actions in this rite to stand on their own. Although brief, the marriage rite has a richness in its texts and actions. Put your energy into proclaiming your vows and the prayer for the exchange of rings clearly. Pay attention to placing the rings on one another's fingers graciously and visibly. Avoid interrupting the flow of this rite with music or other prayers and actions. The advice from Chapter One is especially pertinent to the marriage rite: give priority to the essentials.

Address and Statement of Intentions

Once the priest or deacon, the best man and maid of honor, and the two of you are in place, the priest or deacon addresses you in these or similar words:

My dear friends, you have come together in this church so that the Lord may seal and strengthen your love in the presence of the Church's minister and this community. In this way you will be strengthened to keep mutual and lasting faith with each other and to carry out the other duties of marriage. And so, in the presence of the Church, I ask you to state your intentions.

He then asks you the following questions:

N. and N., have you come here freely and without reservation to give yourselves to each other in marriage?

You each respond: **We have.**

Will you love and honor each other as man and wife for the rest of your lives?

You each respond: **We will.**

(Will you accept children lovingly from God, and bring them up according to the law of Christ and his Church?

You each respond: **We will.)**

Consent and Exchange of Vows

The priest or deacon then says: **Since it is your intention to enter into marriage, join your right hands, and declare your consent before God and his Church.** You join your right hands and declare your consent (that is, exchange your vows) using one of the following formulas:

1. **I, N. take you, N., to be my wife/husband. I promise to be true to you in good times and in bad, in sickness and in health: I will love you and honor you all the days of my life.**

2. **I, N. take you, N., for my lawful wife/ husband, to have and to hold, from this day forward, for better, for worse, for richer, for poorer, in sickness and in health, until death do us part.**

You may also use one of the following formulas in which the priest or deacon poses the question and you each answer, **I do.**

Language note:
"Husband and wife" could be substituted for "man and wife" in the second question.

3. **N., do you take N. to be your wife/ husband? Do you promise to be true to her/him in good times and in bad, in sickness and in health, to love her/him and to honor her/him all the days of your life? . . . I do.**

4. **N., do you take N. for your lawful wife/ husband, to have and to hold, from this day forward, for better, for worse, for richer, for poorer, in sickness and in health, until death do you part? . . . I do.**

The first two formulas represent a more powerful declaration of your consent, since you address one another directly. Memorizing the formula is not difficult, and it allows you to look at each other as you exchange your vows. If you are nervous about forgetting the formula, write it down on an index card and hold the card as you say the vows.

After you have declared your consent, the priest or deacon says:

You have declared your consent before the Church. May the Lord in his goodness strengthen your consent and fill you both with his blessings. What God has joined, men must not divide.

All respond: **Amen.**

Blessing and Exchange of Rings

The priest or deacon then blesses the rings using one of these prayers:

1. **May the Lord bless + these rings
   which you give to each other
   as the sign of your love and fidelity.**

2. **Lord, bless these rings which we bless +
      in your name.
   Grant that those who wear them**

Language note:
"Men and women must not divide" could be substituted for "men must not divide."

may always have a deep faith in each
    other.
May they do your will
and always live together
in peace, good will, and love.
We ask this through Christ our Lord.

3. Lord,
bless + and consecrate N. and N.
in their love for each other.
May these rings be a symbol
of true faith in each other,
and always remind them of their love.
Through Christ our Lord.

The response in each case is **Amen.** The best
man or maid of honor may hold the rings for
the blessing. As he says the blessing prayer,
the priest or deacon may also sprinkle the
rings with blessed water. Then, the groom
places the bride's ring on her finger, and the
bride places the groom's ring on his finger. As
you each do this, you say the following:

**N., take this ring as a sign of my love and
fidelity. In the name of the Father, and
of the Son, and of the Holy Spirit.**

After you have exchanged the rings, the
priest or deacon may invite the assembly to
applaud as a joyful sign of their approval of
the marriage. If the two of you wish to exchange a kiss at this point, by all means do so!

General Intercessions

The marriage rite concludes with the general intercessions, or prayer of the faithful.
This is a set of prayers specifically directed to
the larger needs of the world, the church and
our communities. Usually, the priest or members of the parish write these prayers for Sunday Mass. For the wedding liturgy, you may
want to write them or, at least, suggest specific

Note: If you will be using form II
or III, the general intercessions
are followed by the nuptial blessing. This is on page 45.

intentions to be included in the prayers. This is a good opportunity to personalize the liturgy, while remembering the needs of others in the midst of the day's joy.

For example, you might want to pray for deceased or sick relatives; friends and relatives who could not be at the wedding; parents, godparents and others who have been influential in your lives; and parish and school communities that you have been part of. These should be balanced with broader concerns such as the poor, homeless and unemployed of the city where the wedding is taking place; church and government officials; and peace among nations. If there are going to be people from Protestant or Orthodox churches at the wedding, you might want to include a prayer for the unity of Christian churches. In the same way, you could include a prayer for non-Christian faith communities if they will be represented in the assembly.

The general intercessions begin with a brief introduction by the priest or deacon. Then, the intentions are announced by a reader. This may be one of the people who read the first or second reading, or it may be someone else. There are ordinarily five or six intentions, each simple and relatively brief. Following each intention, the reader says **Let us pray to the Lord** or **We pray to the Lord**, to which the assembly responds **Lord, hear our prayer**, **Hear us, O Lord** or **Lord, have mercy.** The choice of which formula to use depends on the parish's customs and which formula you think most people will be familiar with. After the last intention, there is a brief period of silent prayer, and, then, the priest or deacon says a concluding prayer which sums up and completes the general intercessions.

The priest or deacon can assist you with the composition of these prayers. Two samples are also provided in the back of this book as a guide.

WEDDING GIFTS

Wedding gifts are a very concrete way for people to express their congratulations and best wishes to you as you begin your marriage. Whether it is a unique crystal bowl or the third toaster you've received, each gift is a symbol of the people who gave it and of their love and concern for you. Long after the wedding day, the gifts remind you of these people and help you to recapture the joy of the day.

Gifts also play an important part in the liturgy of the eucharist. At Sunday Mass, three gifts are brought forward: bread, wine and a collection of money. The bread and wine become the basic elements of the eucharistic meal, while the money supports the parish's activities, particularly outreach to those in need. Each of these gifts represents the members of the assembly and their participation in the eucharist and the social mission of the church, the two mutual dimensions of the Christian life.

Because of the importance of gifts in weddings and in the liturgy, two suggestions are offered for your consideration as you prepare the wedding liturgy:

(1) Friends and relatives are often exceedingly generous at weddings. You may already be overwhelmed by the outpouring of gifts.

continued

LITURGY OF THE EUCHARIST
(Weddings within Mass only)

The liturgy of the eucharist at a wedding is celebrated in the same way as it is at Sunday Mass with one exception: the addition of the nuptial blessing before communion. There are also options for the prayers of this part of the liturgy that are specifically related to marriage.

Preparation of the Gifts

After the general intercessions, the assembly is seated and the bread and wine for the eucharist are brought to the altar by two or three people from the assembly. Ideally, you want to choose people who are not fulfilling other special roles such as usher or reader. For example, godparents or other significant people in your lives who are otherwise not serving in a special liturgical ministry at the wedding, might be delighted to be asked to do this. They simply walk to the place where the bread and wine have been set out before Mass, pick up a container of bread or wine, and walk in a simple procession to the altar, where they hand the bread and wine to the priest. Then, they return to their seats. They do not need to bow or genuflect.

The priest receives the bread and wine and says a silent prayer of blessing. Then, he says a prayer over the gifts using one of the following:

1. **Lord,**
    accept our offerings
    for this newly-married couple, N. and N.
    By your love and providence you have
    brought them together;
    now bless them all the days of their
    married life.
    We ask this through Christ our Lord.

2. **Lord,**
   accept the gifts we offer you
   on this happy day.
   In your fatherly love
   watch over and protect N. and N.
   whom you have united in marriage.

   We ask this through Christ our Lord.

3. **Lord,**
   hear our prayers
   and accept the gifts we offer for N. and N.
   Today you have made them one in the
   sacrament of marriage.
   May the mystery of Christ's unselfish love,
   which we celebrate in this eucharist,
   increase their love for you and for each
   other.

   We ask this through Christ our Lord.

The response in each case is: **Amen.**

The Eucharistic Prayer

All stand and the priest begins the eucharistic prayer, or prayer of thanksgiving, with the following dialogue:

Priest: **The Lord be with you.**
All: **And also with you.**

Priest: **Lift up your hearts.**
All: **We lift them up to the Lord.**

Priest: **Let us give thanks to the Lord our God.**
All: **It is right to give him thanks and praise.**

The eucharistic prayer continues as the priest says one of the following prefaces:

1. **Father, all-powerful and ever-living God,**
   we do well always and everywhere to give
   you thanks.
   By this sacrament your grace unites man
   and woman
   in an unbreakable bond of love and peace.

Wedding Gifts *continued*

Some couples have found an equally generous way to respond to this outpouring of gifts by making a gift of their own to the needy in their area. If, for example, you have received the infamous duplicate toasters, why not give one to a soup kitchen? If you have received money, perhaps you could make a donation to the parish's social outreach committee. Such a gift on your part would serve the same function as the collection of money at Sunday Mass. It is an opportunity to share the joy of your wedding with those who are in need.

(2) In the early centuries of Christianity, people brought bread and wine for Mass from their homes. The wedding liturgy offers a marvelous opportunity to renew this ancient custom. You or a member of your family could provide a bottle of wine for the eucharist. Perhaps one of your relatives is a good cook and is anxious to do something to help with the wedding preparations. Why not ask that person to bake the bread? Here is a recipe that is consistent with current church regulations for the bread used at Mass:

Preheat oven to 350.

Ingredients:
2½ cups whole wheat flour
½ cup unbleached white flour
1¼ cups lukewarm water
(110 degrees)
Mix all the ingredients together in a bowl until all the flour is gathered together. Place on the counter and knead for about 5 or 6 minutes. The dough will be on the stiff side, so there is not a great need for very much extra flour to facilitate kneading.

continued

41

Wedding Gifts *continued*

Kneading is most important to prevent puffing or ballooning.

When the dough is smooth and pliable, after kneading, form dough into a ball and let rest for about 5 minutes, covered with a dampened cloth, to prevent a crust from forming.

Divide the dough in half, and roll each half to an eight inch diameter and about ¼ inch thick.

Lightly grease a cookie sheet. Bake the bread immediately upon completion of rolling out. Bake for about 16 or 17 minutes. The bread should not brown, so the color will remain pretty much the same but will lighten somewhat. It must not be overbaked, as some moisture is needed to retain the proper texture.

Cool and wrap in plastic or foil and freeze until a few hours before using.

This recipe produces two 8 inch round loaves, which is enough bread for about one hundred at communion.

Language note:
In preface #2, the following substitution can be made in the second paragraph: "You restored *men and women* to grace...," "You gave *them* a share in the divine life through *their* union with Christ. You made *them* heirs of Christ's eternal glory."

You have designed the chaste love of husband and wife
for the increase both of the human family
and of your own family born in baptism.

You are the loving Father of the world of nature;
you are the loving Father of the new creation of grace.
In Christian marriage you bring together the two orders of creation:
nature's gift of children enriches the world
and your grace enriches also your Church.

Through Christ the choirs of angels
and all the saints
praise and worship your glory.
May our voices blend with theirs
as we join in their unending hymn:

2. Father, all-powerful and ever-living God,
    we do well always and everywhere to give you thanks
    through Jesus Christ our Lord.

    Through him you entered into a new covenant with your people.
    You restored man to grace in the saving mystery of redemption.
    You gave him a share in the divine life through his union with Christ.
    You made him an heir of Christ's eternal glory.

    This outpouring of love in the new covenant of grace
    is symbolized in the marriage covenant
    that seals the love of husband and wife
    and reflects your divine plan of love.

    And so, with the angels and all the saints in heaven
    we proclaim your glory
    and join in their unending hymn of praise:

3. **Father, all-powerful and ever-living God,
we do well always and everywhere to give
you thanks.**

**You created man in love to share your
divine life.
We see his high destiny in the love of
husband and wife,
which bears the imprint of your own
divine love.**

**Love is man's origin,
love is his constant calling,
love is his fulfillment in heaven.**

**The love of man and woman
is made holy in the sacrament of marriage,
and becomes the mirror of your everlasting love.**

**Through Christ the choirs of angels
and all the saints
praise and worship your glory.
May our voices blend with theirs
as we join in their unending hymn:**

Language note:
In preface #3, the following sub-
stitutions could be made in the
second and third paragraphs.
"You created *us* in love," "We see
our high destiny," "Love is *our*
origin, love is *our* constant calling, love is *our* fulfillment in
heaven."

After the preface, all join in the following
prayer (sung or spoken):

**Holy, holy, holy Lord, God of power and
might,
heaven and earth are full of your glory.
Hosanna in the highest.
Blessed is he who comes in the name of
the Lord.
Hosanna in the highest.**

Then, the priest continues with the rest of the
eucharistic prayer. After the "Holy, holy"
prayer, it is customary in many parishes in the
United States for the assembly to kneel. The
couple and any other ministers who are in the
sanctuary (the area immediately adjacent to
the altar) may remain standing. This is an appropriate gesture of praise during the eucharistic prayer and, on a practical note, avoids the
need for kneelers in the sanctuary.

43

There are several optional texts for the eucharistic prayer, each of them too lengthy to reprint here. If you would like to see a copy of these prayers, ask the priest in one of your preparatory meetings with him.

In the middle of the eucharistic prayer, the priest says: **Let us proclaim the mystery of faith.** The assembly responds by singing (or saying) the memorial acclamation. There are four options for this acclamation:

1. **Christ has died,
    Christ is risen,
    Christ will come again.**

2. **Dying you destroyed our death,
    rising you restored our life.
    Lord Jesus, come in glory.**

3. **When we eat this bread and drink this cup,
    we proclaim your death, Lord Jesus,
    until you come in glory.**

4. **Lord, by your cross and resurrection
    you have set us free.
    You are the Savior of the world.**

The eucharistic prayer ends with the following:

Priest: **Through him,
with him,
in him,
in the unity of the Holy Spirit,
all glory and honor is yours,
almighty Father,
for ever and ever.**

The assembly responds by singing (or saying): **Amen.**

The Lord's Prayer

The Lord's Prayer, or "Our Father," is the most basic Christian prayer. Especially in the wedding liturgy, it serves a most important function by uniting worshippers from various Christian churches in a common prayer. It is introduced by the priest or deacon.

Presider: **Let us pray with confidence to the Father in the words our Savior gave us:**

All: **Our Father, who art in heaven, hallowed be thy name; thy kingdom come; thy will be done on earth as it is in heaven. Give us this day our daily bread; and forgive us our trespasses as we forgive those who trespass against us; and lead us not into temptation, but deliver us from evil.**

The prayer that normally follows the Lord's Prayer in the Mass ("Deliver us, Lord, from every evil . . . ") is omitted in the wedding liturgy. Although not mentioned in the *Rite of Marriage*, it would be appropriate, as well as a sign of hospitality and respect, to instead conclude the Lord's Prayer with the traditional ecumenical ending, or "doxology," if there are going to be Christians from other churches at the wedding:

All: **. . . deliver us from evil. For thine is the kingdom, and the power, and the glory, for ever and ever. Amen.**

Nuptial Blessing

There are two blessings of the couple in the wedding liturgy: the nuptial blessing and the final blessing. When the wedding is celebrated within Mass (form I), the nuptial blessing follows the Lord's Prayer. When the wedding is celebrated outside of Mass (form II or III), the nuptial blessing follows the general intercessions, and the Lord's Prayer follows the nuptial blessing.

The priest or deacon faces the couple and prays one of the following options for the nuptial blessing:

Note:

In option #1 for the nuptial blessing, two of the three following paragraphs may be omitted: "Father, by your power . . . ," "Father, you have made . . . ," "Father, by your plan . . . ," keeping only the one paragraph which corresponds to the readings you have chosen.

Language note:

"Humanity" could be substituted for "mankind" in the second paragraph of nuptial blessing #1.

1. **My dear friends, let us turn to the Lord and pray**
   that he will bless with his grace
   this woman (or N.)
   now married in Christ to this man (or N.)
   and that (through the sacrament of the body and blood of Christ,)
   he will unite in love the couple he has joined in this holy bond.

   Father, by your power, you have made everything out of nothing.
   In the beginning you created the universe
   and made mankind in your own likeness.
   You gave man the constant help of woman
   so that man and woman should no longer be two, but one flesh,
   and you teach us that what you have united may never be divided.

   Father, you have made the union of man and woman so holy a mystery that it symbolizes the marriage of Christ and his Church.

   Father, by your plan man and woman are united,
   and married life has been established
   as the one blessing that was not forfeited by original sin
   or washed away in the flood.

   Look with love upon this woman, your daughter,
   now joined to her husband in marriage.
   She asks your blessing.
   Give her the grace of love and peace.
   May she always follow the example of the holy women
   whose praises are sung in the scriptures.

May her husband put his trust in her
and recognize that she is his equal
and the heir with him to the life of grace.
May he always honor her and love her
as Christ loves his bride, the Church.

Father, keep them always true to your
   commandments.
Keep them faithful in marriage
and let them be living examples of
   Christian life.

Give them the strength which comes
   from the gospel
so that they may be witnesses of Christ to
   others.
(Bless them with children
and help them to be good parents.
May they live to see their children's
   children.) _this life here on earth_
And, after a ~~happy old age,~~
grant them fullness of life with the saints
in the kingdom of heaven.

We ask this through Christ our Lord.

2. Let us pray to the Lord for N. and N.
    who come to God's altar at the beginning
       of their married life
    so that they may always be united in love
       for each other
    (as now they share in the body and blood
       of Christ).

    Holy Father, you created mankind in
       your own image
    and made man and woman to be joined
       as husband and wife
    in union of body and heart
    and so fulfill their mission in this world.

    Father, to reveal the plan of your love,
    you made the union of husband and wife
    an image of the covenant between you
       and your people.

    In the fulfillment of this sacrament,
    the marriage of Christian man and woman
    is a sign of the marriage between Christ

Note:
   In option #2 for the nuptial
blessing, either the paragraph
beginning with "Holy Father,
you created mankind..." or the
paragraph beginning with
"Father, to reveal the plan of
your love..." may be omitted,
keeping only the paragraph
which corresponds to the readings you have chosen.

Language note:
   "Humanity" could be substituted for "mankind" in the
second paragraph of nuptial
blessing #2.

and the Church.
Father, stretch out your hand, and bless
   N. and N.

Lord,
grant that as they begin to live this
   sacrament
they may share with each other the gifts
   of your love
and become one in heart and mind
as witnesses to your presence in their
   marriage.
Help them to create a home together
(and give them children to be formed by
   the gospel
and to have a place in your family).

Give your blessing to N., your daughter,
so that she may be a good wife (and
   mother),
caring for the home,
faithful in love for her husband,
generous and kind.
Give your blessings to N., your son,
so that he may be a faithful husband
(and a good father).

Father, grant that as they come together
   to your table on earth,
so they may one day have the joy of
   sharing your feast in heaven.

We ask this through Christ our Lord.

3. My dear friends, let us ask God
   for his continued blessings upon this
     bridegroom and his bride (or N.
     and N.).

Holy Father, creator of the universe,
maker of man and woman in your own
   likeness,
source of blessing for married life,
we humbly pray to you for this woman
who today is united with her husband in
   this sacrament of marriage.

May your fullest blessing come upon her
   and her husband

so that they may together rejoice in your
   gift of married love
(and enrich your Church with their
   children).

Lord,
may they both praise you when they are
   happy
and turn to you in their sorrows.
May they be glad that you help them in
   their work
and know that you are with them in their
   need.
May they pray to you in the community
   of the Church,
and be your witnesses in the world.
May they reach old age in the company of
   their friends,
and come at last to the kingdom of
   heaven.

We ask this through Christ our Lord.

The response in each case is: **Amen.**

Sign of Peace

The priest faces the assembly and says: **Let us offer each other the sign of peace.** All exchange a handshake, kiss or other gesture of peace, saying: **The peace of Christ be with you.**

Breaking of the Bread

After the sign of peace, those who will serve as communion ministers come into the sanctuary and stand near the altar. They may bring the additional containers for the distribution of the bread and cups for the distribution of the wine to the altar, and assist the priest in dividing the bread among the several containers and pouring the wine into the several cups. During this time, the assembly sings (or says) the following:

WHO MAY RECEIVE COMMUNION?

To share in eating the bread and drinking from the cup of the eucharist is the preeminent sign of unity for Christians. It is the most intimate experience of union with God and with one another in the church's tradition. This is the meaning of the word "communion." Unfortunately, the current situation among Christians is one of disunity. There are Protestant, Orthodox and Roman Catholic churches, rather than one Christian Church. The guidelines for communion in the Catholic Church reflect this situation: since the various churches are not united, it would be a false sign for Catholics to share the eucharist with non-Catholics, a practice called "inter-communion."

It is precisely because inter-communion is not permitted that a wedding Mass is not encouraged when a Catholic marries a non-Catholic. The eucharist would, in these weddings, be a sign of disunity at a time when the stress is on unity. A wedding outside of Mass is just as complete and is a more honest choice when a Catholic marries a non-Catholic.

The question of who may receive communion also arises in weddings involving two Catholics but where a number of non-

continued

Lamb of God, you take away the sins of the world: have mercy on us.
Lamb of God, you take away the sins of the world: have mercy on us.
Lamb of God, you take away the sins of the world: grant us peace.

Communion

The priest introduces the communion rite with the following:

Priest: **This is the Lamb of God who takes away the sins of the world. Happy are those who are called to his supper.**

All: **Lord, I am not worthy to receive you, but only say the word and I shall be healed.**

The priest eats the bread and drinks from the cup. Then, he offers the bread and wine to the communion ministers and to each of you, saying, **The body/blood of Christ**, to which you respond **Amen.** Once you have received the bread and wine, the priest and communion ministers begin to distribute the bread and wine to the assembly. During this time, a song or instrumental music may be used. (See Chapter Four for specific suggestions.)

Communion under the forms of both bread and wine, or "communion under both kinds," is preferred to communion under the form of bread alone. This ancient practice, which was reintroduced for regular use in the United States in 1984, is a fuller response to the words of Christ at the Last Supper: "take and eat . . . take and drink." Many parishes have now adopted this practice for all Sunday Masses. The wedding liturgy offers an especially appropriate opportunity to celebrate the eucharistic banquet in its fullest form.

If the communion ministers for your wedding liturgy have not served in this role before, it would be wise to ask them to attend the rehearsal. The priest can explain the role to them at that time. To determine how many communion ministers you will need, plan on one communion minister of the bread and two communion ministers of the cup (the wine) for every seventy-five people in the assembly. (The presiding priest should be counted as one of the ministers.) This will allow for a reverent, yet not extended, distribution of communion.

Prayer after Communion

After communion, a period of slient prayer may be observed, or a post-communion song may be sung (see Chapter Four). Then, all stand and the priest says one of the following prayers:

1. **Lord,**
   in your love
   you have given us this eucharist
   to unite us with one another and with
   ** you.**
   As you have made N. and N.
   one in this sacrament of marriage
   (and in the sharing of the one bread and
   ** the one cup),**
   so now make them one in love for each
   ** other.**

   We ask this through Christ our Lord.

2. **Lord,**
   we who have shared the food of your
   ** table**
   pray for our friends N. and N.,
   whom you have joined together in
   ** marriage.**
   Keep them close to you always.
   May their love for each other
   proclaim to all the world
   their faith in you.

   We ask this through Christ our Lord.

Catholics will be in the assembly. Two things should be kept in mind here: (1) since inter-communion is not permitted, it is not appropriate to invite non-Catholics to receive the eucharist at a wedding Mass; (2) at the same time, it is inappropriate and inhospitable to announce that non-Catholics may not receive the eucharist at a wedding Mass. In other words, the current church regulations should be respected, but there is no need to make announcements about the regulations within the liturgy or in the program. Ultimately, the decision to receive the eucharist always rests with the individual person.

If the regulations concerning inter-communion are disturbing, they should be. They reflect a deeper scandal: the disunity of the Christian Church that Jesus sought to be one. It's all the more reason to pray for the unity of the church in the general intercessions and to pay special attention to making non-Catholics feel welcome at your wedding liturgy.

3. **Almighty God,**
   may the sacrifice we have offered
   and the eucharist we have shared
   strengthen the love of N. and N.,
   and give us all your fatherly aid.

   We ask this through Christ our Lord.

The response in each case is: **Amen.**

CONCLUDING RITES

Final Blessing

The priest or deacon says, **The Lord be with you**, to which all respond, **And also with you.** Then, the priest or deacon says one of the following blessing prayers:

1. **God the eternal Father keep you in love**
   with each other,
   so that the peace of Christ may stay with
   you
   and be always in your home.
   All respond: **Amen.**
   May (your children bless you,)
   your friends console you
   and all men live in peace with you.
   All respond: **Amen.**
   May you always bear witness to the love
   of God in this world
   so that the afflicted and the needy
   will find in you generous friends,
   and welcome you into the joys of heaven.
   All respond: **Amen.**
   And may almighty God bless you all,
   the Father, and the Son, + and the Holy
   Spirit.
   All respond: **Amen.**

2. **May God, the almighty Father,**
   give you his joy
   and bless you (in your children).
   All respond: **Amen.**

May the only Son of God have mercy on
you
and help you in good times and in bad.
All respond: **Amen.**
May the Holy Spirit of God
always fill your hearts with his love.
All respond: **Amen.**
And may almighty God bless you all,
the Father, and the Son, + and the Holy
Spirit.
All respond: **Amen.**

3. May the Lord Jesus, who was a guest at
the wedding in Cana,
bless you and your families and friends.
All respond: **Amen.**
May Jesus, who loved his Church to the
end,
always fill your hearts with his love.
All respond: **Amen.**
May he grant that, as you believe in his
resurrection,
so you may wait for him in joy and hope.
All respond: **Amen.**
And may almighty God bless you all,
the Father, and the Son, + and the Holy
Spirit.
All respond: **Amen.**

4. May almighty God, with his Word of
blessing, unite your hearts in the
never-ending bond of pure love.
All respond: **Amen.**
May your children bring you happiness,
and may your generous love for them
be returned to you, many times over.
All respond: **Amen.**
May the peace of Christ live always in
your hearts and in your home.
May you have true friends to stand by
you, both in joy and in sorrow.
May you be ready and willing to help and
comfort all who come to you in need.
And may the blessings promised to the
compassionate be yours in abundance.
All respond: **Amen.**

May you find happiness and satisfaction in your work. May daily problems never cause you undue anxiety, nor the desire for earthly possessions dominate your lives. But may your hearts' first desire be always the good things waiting for you in the life of heaven.
All respond: **Amen.**

May the Lord bless you with many happy years together, so that you may enjoy the rewards of a good life. And after you have served him loyally in his kingdom on earth, may he welcome you to his eternal kingdom in heaven.
All respond: **Amen.**

And may almighty God bless you all, the Father, and the Son, + and the Holy Spirit.
All respond: **Amen.**

Solemn blessings, such as these, which are interspersed with "Amen" responses by the assembly, are unfamiliar to many worshippers, including Roman Catholics. As a result, few people make the "Amen" responses during the blessing. In light of this, two suggestions are offered: (a) have someone — the leader of song or the two of you — lead the "Amen" responses from a microphone; or (b) omit all but the final "Amen" response.

Although not mentioned in the *Rite of Marriage*, a custom in some parishes for the final blessing is to ask the assembly to join the priest or deacon in blessing the couple. To do this, the two of you face the assembly, and the priest or deacon stands at the head of the assembly facing you. All extend their right arm toward you and recite the blessing prayer with the priest or deacon. If you choose to do this, be sure to print the text of the blessing in the program. (See Sample Programs #2 and #3 at the back of the book for examples of this.) The final sentence of the blessing ("And may almighty God bless you all ... ") is always said by the priest or deacon alone, as it is addressed to the entire assembly.

Dismissal

After the Final Blessing, the priest says one of the following:

1. **Go in the peace of Christ.**

2. **The Mass is ended, go in peace.**

3. **Go in peace to love and serve the Lord.**

The response in each case is: **Thanks be to God.**

Recessional

The recessional is a simple procession out of the church. The two of you go first, followed by the ushers and bridesmaids. The priest or deacon may follow you, or he may remain in the sanctuary. An upbeat, festive piece of music is most effective to accompany this simple procession and to serve as a bridge to the continuation of the wedding celebration at the reception (see Chapter Four).

CHAPTER THREE

THE READINGS:
THE LECTIONARY FOR MARRIAGE

Selecting the scripture readings to be proclaimed at your wedding liturgy ought to be done with careful reflection and discussion. It is an opportunity to share with one another some of the deepest values you hold. Use the readings to review and ponder what Christian marriage and Christian life mean to you.

It is customary to have three scripture readings in the wedding liturgy: one from the Hebrew scriptures (Old Testament), one from the writings of the apostles, and one from the Gospels. For pastoral reasons which might be discussed with the priest or deacon, one of the first two readings may sometimes be omitted. Between the first and second readings, a psalm is sung. If it is not possible to sing the psalm, it may be recited. (The psalms for weddings and information about appropriate musical settings are in Chapter Four.)

Some couples ask about the possibility of using readings from sources other than the scriptures in the wedding liturgy. While such readings may reflect valuable insights into marriage, they are best used outside of the liturgy. The readings in the wedding liturgy are limited to those that the church holds to be the Word of God, that is, the scriptures.

The gospel is always proclaimed by either the priest or deacon who presides at your wedding. This is the only scripture reading that he should read. The other readings should be proclaimed by other people, either readers from the parish or people chosen by you. Take special care that the people you choose as readers have a gift for reading in public or will work hard to proclaim the text well. Planning the roles friends and relatives will exercise in your wedding liturgy can be tricky business indeed. You don't want to hurt feelings, but neither do you want to embarrass someone who may not be gifted with an ability to read well in public.

Once you have chosen the readers, get the text of the readings to them in plenty of time to practice. Ideally, one person should proclaim the first reading, and someone else the second reading. If, however, you can only identify one good reader among the people who will be at your wedding, this person may do both readings. At the rehearsal, be sure that the readers have a chance to read from the lectern they will use, with the amplification system turned on. Do not allow the readers to read from a simple sheet of paper or from this book during the liturgy. The Word of God should be in a dignified and substantial binding. The parish will have a bound copy of the scripture readings for liturgy (called a lectionary), and the priest or deacon can locate the readings you have chosen.

After the wedding is over, you might want to hold onto this book to use for discussion, sharing of insights, and praying together in the months and years ahead. Certain readings which might not appeal to you now might hold wonderful insights for you later as your experience of marriage deepens.

OPTIONS FOR THE FIRST READING
from the Hebrew scriptures (Old Testament)

OT-1: Genesis 1, 26-28. 31

God said: "Let us make man in our image, after our likeness. Let them have dominion over the fish of the sea, the birds of the air, and the cattle, and over all the wild animals and all the creatures that crawl on the ground."
God created man in his image:
 in the divine image he created him;
 male and female he created them.
God blessed them, saying: "Be fertile and multiply; fill the earth and subdue it. Have dominion over the fish of the sea, the birds of the air, and all the living things that move on the earth." God looked at everything he had made, and he found it very good.

There are two accounts of the creation of the world and of humankind in Genesis. In this first account, the creation of man and woman represents the climax of creation; they are created in the image and likeness of God, man and woman together constituting this image and likeness of God. The wonderful dignity of man and woman is taught in this story as well as their complementarity, the essence of the gift of sexuality which God pronounced very good. Psalm 8, although not suggested for weddings in the lectionary, would be a beautiful and appropriate responsorial psalm after this reading:

Psalm 8, 4-5. 6-7. 8-9

ACKNOWLEDGMENT

Two books were particularly helpful in the preparation of the commentary that follows each of the readings: *Preaching the Lectionary* by Reginald H. Fuller (Collegeville MN: The Liturgical Press, 1984) and *Commentaries on the Ritual Readings* by Robert Crotty and John Barry Ryan (New York NY: Pueblo Publishing Co., 1982).

BEGINNINGS AND ENDINGS

When scripture readings are proclaimed during the liturgy, they are introduced and concluded by certain phrases. Before the reading, the reader says "A reading from the book of Genesis" or "from the book of Tobit" or "from the letter of Paul to the Ephesians," depending on the individual reading. The reader should establish eye contact with the assembly before and after this phrase, before proceeding into the body of the text.

After the reading, the reader says "This is the Word of the Lord," to which the assembly responds "Thanks be to God." Once again, the reader should pause briefly after the last line of the reading and look up at the assembly before saying this phrase. The reader also remains in place at the lectern until the assembly has made its response. It is the practice in some parishes for the reader to remain at the lectern with head bowed after the response to give all a few moments to reflect on the reading that has just been proclaimed.

Response: O Lord, our God,
how wonderful your name in all the earth!

When I behold your heavens, the work of your fingers,the moon and the stars which you set in place —
What is man that you should be mindful of him, or the son of man that you should care for him?
Response: O Lord, our God,
how wonderful your name in all the earth!

You have made him little less than the angels, and crowned him with glory and honor.
You have given him rule over the works of your hands, putting all things under his feet:
Response: O Lord, our God,
how wonderful your name in all the earth!

All sheep and oxen,
yes, and the beasts of the field,
The birds of the air, the fishes of the sea,
and whatever swims the paths of the seas.
Response: O Lord, our God,
how wonderful your name in all the earth!

OT-2:   Genesis 2, 18-24

The LORD God said: "It is not good for the man to be alone. I will make a suitable partner for him." So the LORD God formed out of the ground various wild animals and various birds of the air, and he brought them to the man to see what he would call them; whatever the man called each of them would be its name. The man gave names to all the cattle, all the birds of the air, and all the wild animals; but none proved to be the suitable partner for the man.

So the LORD God cast a deep sleep on the man, and while he was asleep, he took out one of his ribs and closed up its place with flesh. The LORD God then

built up into a woman the rib that he had taken from the man. When he brought her to the man, the man said:

"This one, at last, is bone of my bones
and flesh of my flesh;
This one shall be called 'woman,'
for out of 'her man' this one has been taken."

That is why a man leaves his father and mother and clings to his wife, and the two of them become one body.

This is the second and, according to today's standards, less popular account of creation. In the past, this description of the creation of the first woman from the rib of man was sometimes used to point up the subordination of woman to man as his helpmate. But contemporary scholars point out that the Hebrew word for help does not indicate subordination. It is used, for example, of God as the helper of Israel. The New American version of the Bible, which is used in this book, translates helpmate properly as partner. This story might be used to preach on the sanctity of physical creation, with particular emphasis on the sanctity of human sexuality. Man and woman in marriage are to be one flesh; so it has been ordained by God.

OT-3:   Genesis 24, (34-47.) 48-51. 58-67

The servant of Abraham said to Laban: ("I am Abraham's servant. The LORD has blessed my master so abundantly that he has become a wealthy man; he has given him flocks and herds, silver and gold, male and female slaves, and camels and asses. My master's wife Sarah bore a son to my master in her old age, and he has given him everything he owns. My master put me under oath, saying: 'You shall not procure a wife for my son among the

THE LANGUAGE OF THE READINGS

Some of the names that appear in certain readings are a real challange to one's pronunciation skills. For this reason, a guide to pronunciation is included in the margin next to some of the more unfamiliar names.

Also in the margin are occasional suggestions for alternative language that does not exclude women. For example, "brothers" can easily be changed to "brothers and sisters" and "men" can be changed to "all" when it is clear that people in general are intended, not just men.

Pronunciation note:
Laban = LAY - b'n

Note: The verses in parentheses in OT-3 are not part of the reading as it appears in the lectionary. They are reprinted here, as the commentary indicates, to set the context for the story.

daughters of the Canaanites in whose land I live; instead, you shall go to my father's house, to my own relatives, to get a wife for my son.' When I asked my master, 'What if the woman will not follow me?' he replied: 'The LORD, in whose presence I have always walked, will send his messenger with you and make your errand successful, and so you will get a wife for my son from my own kindred of my father's house. Then you shall be released from my ban. If you visit my kindred and they refuse you, then, too, you shall be released from my ban.'

"When I came to the spring today, I prayed: 'LORD, God of my master Abraham, may it be your will to make successful the errand I am engaged on! While I stand here at the spring, if I say to a young woman who comes out to draw water, Please give me a little water from your jug, and she answers, Not only may you have a drink, but I will give water to your camels, too — let her be the woman whom the LORD has decided upon for my master's son.'

"I had scarcely finished saying this prayer to myself when Rebekah came out with a jug on her shoulder. After she went down to the spring and drew water, I said to her, 'Please let me have a drink.' She quickly lowered the jug she was carrying and said, 'Take a drink, and let me bring water for your camels, too.' So I drank, and she watered the camels also. When I asked her, 'Whose daughter are you?' she answered, 'The daughter of Bethuel, son of Nahor, born to Nahor by Milcah.' So I put the ring on her nose and the bracelets on her wrists.) Then I bowed down in worship to the LORD, blessing the LORD, the God of my master Abraham, who had led me on the right road to obtain the daughter of my master's kinsman for his son. If, there-

Pronunciation notes:

Bethuel = BETH - oo - el

Nahor = NAY - hore

Milcah = MIL - cah

fore, you have in mind to show true loyalty to my master, let me know; but if not, let me know that, too. I can then proceed accordingly."

Laban and his household said in reply: "This thing comes from the LORD; we can say nothing to you either for or against it. Here is Rebekah, ready for you; take her with you, that she may become the wife of your master's son, as the LORD has said."

So they called Rebekah and asked her, "Do you wish to go with this man?" She answered, "I do." At this they allowed their sister Rebekah and her nurse to take leave, along with Abraham's servant and his men. Invoking a blessing on Rebekah, they said:
"Sister, may you grow
   into thousands of myriads;
And may your descendants gain
      possession
   of the gates of their enemies!"
Then Rebekah and her maids started out; they mounted their camels and followed the man. So the servant took Rebekah and went on his way.

Meanwhile Isaac had gone from Beerlahairoi and was living in the region of the Negeb. One day toward evening he went out . . . in the field, and as he looked about, he noticed that camels were approaching. Rebekah, too, was looking about, and when she saw him, she alighted from her camel and asked the servant, "Who is the man out there, walking through the fields toward us?" "That is my master," replied the servant. Then she covered herself with her veil.

The servant recounted to Isaac all the things he had done. Then Isaac took Rebekah into his tent; he married her, and thus she became his wife. In his love for her Isaac found solace after the death of his mother Sarah.

Pronunciation notes:
Isaac = EYE - zik

Beerlahairoi =
   BEE - er - luh - HAY - roy

Negeb = NEH - geb

Many of the people at your wedding will not be familiar with this story. In order for it to make sense, the reader should start at verse 34 of chapter 24. These additional verses have been included in parentheses. When the whole story is read, it is a beautiful reading which emphasizes how Yahweh proved his fidelity by providing an appropriate wife for Abraham's son, Isaac. The first of the three nuptial blessings from the *Rite of Marriage* (see page 46) mentions the holy women whose praises were sung in the scriptures. Rebekah was one of those holy women. God's fidelity to the married couple could be stressed as well as the importance of the companionship and consolation husband and wife can offer each other in difficult times. So it should be, as Rebekah consoled Isaac after the loss of his mother.

OT-4:   Tobit 7, 9-10. 11-15

Tobiah said to Raphael, "Brother Azariah, ask Raguel to let me marry my kinswoman Sarah." Raguel overheard the words; so he said to the boy: "Eat and drink and be merry tonight, for no man is more entitled to marry my daughter Sarah than you, brother. Besides, not even I have the right to give her to anyone but you, because you are my closest relative. But I will explain the situation to you very frankly. She is yours according to the decree of the Book of Moses. Your marriage to her has been decided in heaven! Take your kinswoman; from now on you are her love, and she is your beloved. She is yours today and ever after. And tonight, son, may the LORD of heaven prosper you both. May he grant you mercy and peace." Then Raguel called his daughter Sarah, and she came to him. He took her by the hand and gave

her to Tobiah with the words: "Take her according to the law. According to the decree written in the Book of Moses she is your wife. Take her and bring her back safely to your father. And may the God of heaven grant both of you peace and prosperity." He then called her mother and told her to bring a scroll, so that he might draw up a marriage contract stating that he gave Sarah to Tobiah as his wife according to the decree of the Mosaic law. Her mother brought the scroll, and he drew up the contract, to which they affixed their seals.

Afterward they began to eat and drink.

Pronunciation note:
Mosaic = moe - ZAY - ik

This and the following reading from Tobit are parts of the same story. But as in the previous reading from Genesis, one needs to know something of the story of the Book of Tobit to grasp the full significance of these selections from the account. Tobit, a devout and charitable man, lived in exile at Ninevah. His kinsman Raguel lived at Ecbatana. Each had a serious problem. Tobit was blind and Raguel's daughter Sarah had seven bridegrooms in succession killed on the wedding night by the demon Asmodeus. God heard the prayers of Tobit and Sarah; he sent Tobit's son Tobiah to Raguel, married him to Sarah (and he was *not* killed on the wedding night) and gave him a cure for his father's blindness. The story is a lesson in hope, perseverance and trust in God even in seemingly hopeless circumstances. The story has a certain human warmth and gentle humor. Tobit's talk of following the law of Moses refers to the patriarchal custom of keeping marriage within the clan. Making God and trust in God the foundation of your marriage is a formula for success.

maybe **On the wedding night Sarah got up, and she and Tobiah started to pray and beg that deliverance might be theirs. He began with these words:**

"Blessed are you, O God of our fathers;
 praised be your name forever and ever.
Let the heavens and all your creation
 praise you forever.
You made Adam and you gave him his
 wife Eve to be his help and support;
 and from these two the human race
 descended.
You said, 'It is not good for the man to
 be alone; let us make him a partner
 like himself.'
Now, LORD, you know that I take this
 wife of mine not because of lust,
 but for a noble purpose.
Call down your mercy on me and on her,
 and allow us to live together to a
 happy old age."

If one knows of Sarah's experience on her seven previous wedding nights, one can understand the urgency of both Sarah's and Tobiah's prayer. It is a lovely scene. Tobiah shows great respect for Sarah in his prayer. God created man and woman to be companions, partners. So he does not take her for any lustful motive, but in singleness of heart. To love each other with singleness of heart is a grace to be sought for in every marriage. And it is one God fully intends to grant, because fidelity and love in marriage are ordained to point to the faithful love of God for us. Marriage is to be a mystery pointing to the mysterious union of Christ with his church (see NT-5).

Song of Songs 2, 8-10. 14. 16; 8, 6-7

> Hark! my lover — here he comes
> springing across the mountains,
> leaping across the hills.
> My lover is like a gazelle
> or a young stag.
> Here he stands behind our wall,
> gazing through the windows,
> peering through the lattices.
> My lover speaks; he says to me,
> "Arise, my beloved, my beautiful one,
> and come!
> O my dove in the clefts of the rock,
> in the secret recesses of the cliff,
> Let me see you,
> let me hear your voice,
> For your voice is sweet,
> and you are lovely."
> My lover belongs to me and I to him.
> (He said to me:)
> Set me as a seal on your heart,
> as a seal on your arm;
> For stern as death is love,
> relentless as the nether world is
> devotion; its flames are a blazing fire.
> Deep waters cannot quench love,
> nor floods sweep it away.

Some commentators, both Jewish and Christian, interpret the Song of Songs, which means "the greatest of all songs," allegorically. That is, they see the relationship of lover and beloved in the poems as pointing to various moments in the love relationship between God and Israel, or between Christ and the church. Other scholars see the book as a collection of hymns to true love sanctified by union. The inclusion of the Song of Songs in the canon of holy scripture leads us to interpret the work as an analogy of the love of God for us; this interpretation also affirms the goodness and sanctity of sexual love. The passionate love of God for us is a mystery as is the passionate love of man and woman. It is as strong as death. The love of God for us in Christ conquered death forever and God's Spirit of love given to us is the guarantee of our living and loving forever.

OT-7:   Sirach 26, 1-4. 13-16

Happy the husband of a good wife;
  twice-lengthened are his days;
A worthy wife brings joy to her husband,
  peaceful and full is his life.
A good wife is a generous gift
  bestowed upon him who fears the LORD;
Be he rich or poor, his heart is content,
  and a smile is ever on his face.
A gracious wife delights her husband,
  her thoughtfulness puts flesh on his
  bones;
A gift from the LORD is her governed
  speech, and her firm virtue is of
  surpassing worth.
Choicest of blessings is a modest wife,
  priceless her chaste person.
Like the sun rising in the LORD's
  heavens, the beauty of a virtuous wife
  is the radiance of her home.

Much of the Book of Sirach consists of advice from a father to his son and includes advice on sex and marriage. No doubt, not many couples today will choose this reading given the viewpoint taken in it. The selection is a description of a good wife from the husband's point of view which seems to place too great an emphasis on her function to provide him happiness. Roles and relationships change in society. But even in the second century before Christ, which is reflected in this reading, the centrality of one's marriage partner in one's life is clearly spelled out. There is a lesson here for us today when often two careers in one household, or the temptation to materialism which financial security and affluence brings, puts serious stresses on marriage relationships and tempts one to think that one's marriage partner is just one among many important things in one's life. That is not the message in Sirach.

OT-8:   Jeremiah 31, 31-32. 33-34

The days are coming, says the LORD, when I will make a new covenant with the house of Israel and the house of Judah. It will not be like the covenant I made with their fathers the day I took them by the hand to lead them forth from the land of Egypt. But this is the covenant which I will make with the house of Israel after those days, says the LORD. I will place my law within them, and write it upon their hearts; I will be their God, and they shall be my people. No longer will they have need to teach their friends and kinsmen how to know the LORD. All, from least to greatest, shall know me, says the LORD.

Pronunciation note:
Jeremiah = jer - eh - MY - uh

For the nomadic peoples of the desert, a covenant was a bond as strong as blood. The welfare of a covenant partner meant as much to you as your own welfare; whenever in need, what is mine is yours, what is yours is mine. The covenant in this reading from Jeremiah is that promised to Israel as the people of God and fulfilled, according to Christian faith, in Christ. If this reading is linked to Ephesians (see NT-5), the relationship between the covenant between God and his people and the marriage covenant can be highlighted. It is the faith of the church that marriage is the privileged place where the covenant of God's love may be most effectively embodied among God's people. Marriage covenant love ought to be a pledge of and an anticipation of the love shown in the kingdom of heaven. Marriage is, in a true sense, a herald announcing that kingdom.

OPTIONS FOR THE SECOND READING
from the New Testament

NT-1:   Romans 8, 31-35. 37-39

maybe

If God is for us, who can be against us? Is it possible that he who did not spare his own Son but handed him over for the sake of us all will not grant us all things besides? Who shall bring a charge against God's chosen ones? God, who justifies? Who shall condemn them? Christ Jesus, who died or rather was raised up, who is at the right hand of God and who intercedes for us?

Who will separate us from the love of Christ? Trial, or distress, or persecution, or hunger, or nakedness, or danger, or the sword? Yet in all this we are more than conquerors because of him who has loved us. For I am certain that neither death nor life, neither angels nor principalities, neither the present nor the future, nor powers, neither height nor depth nor any other creature, will be able to separate us from the love of God that comes to us in Christ Jesus, our Lord.

For Saint Paul, the power of the love of God was demonstrated by the obedient death of Jesus on the cross. The death and resurrection of Jesus was the definitive victory over all of life's troubles including death so that nothing in the future can interfere with God's love for us; nothing can take us out of God's reach. God's powerful and unconditional love is the ideal of love married persons should strive for: first between themselves, then for all their brothers and sisters. While this reading fits well into any series of readings in the marriage lectionary, it might be very fitting after the reading from the Song of Songs (OT-6). It is difficult for humans to imagine the depth and breadth of God's unconditional love for them; we are so conscious of our own limits, our pride and self-centeredness. But we must resist the temptation to model God's love on our own and rather strive to model our love on God's, relying on the Spirit who is love to empower us.

NT-2:   Romans 12, 1-2. 9-18

Brothers, I beg you through the mercy of God to offer your bodies as a living sacrifice holy and acceptable to God, your spiritual worship. Do not conform yourselves to this age but be transformed by the renewal of your mind, so that you may judge what is God's will, what is good, pleasing and perfect.

Your love must be sincere. Detest what is evil, cling to what is good. Love one another with the affection of brothers. Anticipate each other in showing respect. Do not grow slack but be fervent in spirit; he whom you serve is the Lord. Rejoice in hope, be patient under trial, persevere in prayer. Look on the needs of the saints as your own; be generous in offering hospitality. Bless your persecutors; bless and do not curse them. Rejoice with those who rejoice, weep with those who weep. Have the same attitude toward all. Put away ambitious thoughts and associate with those who are lowly. Do not be wise in your own estimation. Never repay injury with injury. See that your conduct is honorable in the eyes of all. If possible, live peaceably with everyone.

Language note:
"Brothers and sisters" could be substituted for "brothers" in both the first and second paragraphs of NT-2.

(Short form: Romans 12, 1-2. 9-13)

Brothers, I beg you through the mercy of God to offer your bodies as a living sacrifice holy and acceptable to God, your spiritual worship. Do not conform yourselves to this age but be transformed by the renewal of your mind so that you may judge what is God's will, what is good, pleasing and perfect.

Your love must be sincere. Detest what is evil, cling to what is good. Love one another with the affection of brothers. Anticipate each other in showing respect. Do not grow slack but be fervent in spirit; he whom you serve is the Lord. Rejoice in hope, be patient under trial, persevere in prayer. Look on the needs of the saints as your own; be generous in offering hospitality.

Paul urges the Christians at Rome to put their beliefs into practice so that their Christian behavior might become a sacrifice to God. He follows this with a warning not to model their lives on the behavior patterns of the world. Married couples would do well to frame this passage on Christian love and pray over it daily. Paul includes hospitality among the qualities Christians should manifest; this is a special virtue of married couples who should not be turned in on themselves, but make their home a place of welcome for others. In our society which encourages expectations of affluent living, our dreams of the future should encompass the welfare of all people, especially the poor, not just our own families.

Pronunciation note:
Corinthians =
cor - IN - thee - enz

NT-3:   I Corinthians 6, 13-15. 17-20

The body is not for immorality; it is for the Lord, and the Lord is for the body.

God, who raised up the Lord, will raise
us also by his power. Do you not see that
your bodies are members of Christ? But
whoever is joined to the Lord becomes
one spirit with him. Shun lewd conduct.
Every other sin a man commits is outside his body, but the fornicator sins
against his own body. You must know
that your body is a temple of the Holy
Spirit, who is within — the Spirit you
have received from God. You are not
your own. You have been purchased, and
at what a price! So glorify God in your
body.

Language note:
"Every other sin one commits"
could be substituted for "every
other sin a man commits."

Do not be put off by Paul's chastening tone;
the passage contains a very important Christian affirmation: the flesh and all material creation is holy and belongs to the Lord. Paul
uses two images to stress the sanctity of the
human body: he reminds the Christians that
their bodies are members of Christ's body and
that they are temples of the Holy Spirit. We are
not our own; we have been bought and paid
for by the life and death of Jesus. There is
evidence that this reading was already in use
in some Christian marriage services in the
sixth century.

NT-4:   1 Corinthians 12, 31—13, 8   *maybe*

Set your hearts on the greater gifts. I will
show you the way which surpasses all the
others. If I speak with human tongues
and angelic as well, but do not have love,
I am a noisy gong, a clanging cymbal. If I
have the gift of prophecy and, with full
knowledge, comprehend all mysteries, if
I have faith great enough to move mountains, but have not love, I am nothing. If
I give everything to feed the poor and

hand over my body to be burned, but have not love, I gain nothing.

Love is patient; love is kind. Love is not jealous, it does not put on airs, it is not snobbish. Love is never rude, it is not self-seeking, it is not prone to anger; neither does it brood over injuries. Love does not rejoice in what is wrong but rejoices with the truth. There is no limit to love's forebearance, to its trust, its hope, its power to endure.

Love never fails.

Paul teaches us that, while talent and knowledge are wonderful gifts, love is the one thing required of us in life. But love is demanding; it encompasses patience, humility, selflessness, courtesy and respect. Love puts good interpretations on what others say and do; it does not resent others' success but rejoices in it and in the truth. Love is ready to forgive, to trust and to endure. Little more need be said about the heart of a marriage relationship. But the source of such a love which is promised to every couple in the sacrament of marriage, can only be God.

Pronunciation note:
Ephesians =
 eh - FEE - shenz

NT-5: Ephesians 5, 2. 21-33

Follow the way of love, even as Christ loved you. He gave himself for us.

Defer to one another out of reverence for Christ.

Wives should be submissive to their husbands as if to the Lord because the husband is head of his wife just as Christ is head of his body the church, as well as its savior. As the church submits to Christ, so wives should submit to their husbands in everything.

Husbands, love your wives, as Christ loved the church. He gave himself up for her to make her holy, purifying her in the bath of water by the power of the word, to present to himself a glorious church, holy and immaculate, without stain or wrinkle or anything of that sort. Husbands should love their wives as they do their own bodies. He who loves his wife loves himself. Observe that no one ever hates his own flesh; no, he nourishes it and takes care of it as Christ cares for the church — for we are members of his body.

"For this reason a man shall leave his
    father and mother,
    and shall cling to his wife,
    and the two shall be made into one."
This is a great foreshadowing; I mean that it refers to Christ and the church. In any case, each one should love his wife as he loves himself, the wife for her part showing respect for her husband.

(Short form: Ephesians 5, 2. 25-32)

Follow the way of love, even as Christ loved you. He gave himself for us.

Husbands, love your wives, as Christ loved the church. He gave himself up for her to make her holy, purifying her in the bath of water by the power of the word, to present to himself a glorious church, holy and immaculate, without stain or wrinkle or anything of that sort. Husbands should love their wives as they do their own bodies. He who loves his wife loves himself. Observe that no one ever hates his own flesh; no, he nourishes it and takes care of it as Christ cares for the church — for we are members of his body.

"For this reason a man shall leave his
    father and mother,
    and shall cling to his wife,
    and the two shall be made into one."
This is a great foreshadowing; I mean that it refers to Christ and the church.

This reading is part of what scholars call a household code. Taken by early Christianity from Hellenistic Judaism, these codes set forth the duties of husbands, wives, parents, children, masters and slaves. In some cases the codes were borrowed almost without change, but this passage in Ephesians added a special elaboration on the meaning of marriage by comparing it to the relation between Christ and his church. The reading reflects the subordinationist pattern of societal relationships in force at that time. Notice, however, that this is *not* the distinctly Christian element in the household code presented here. The Christian community, including our own, is never exempt from cultural conditioning. The inspiring heart of this passage, however, portrays the love of husband and wife as so special that it can be compared analogously to the great love of Christ for the church.

Pronunciation note:
Colossians =
    kuh - LOSH - enz

NT-6:   Colossians 3, 12-17

Because you are God's chosen ones, holy and beloved, clothe yourselves with heartfelt mercy, with kindness, humility, meekness, and patience. Bear with one another; forgive whatever grievances you have against one another. Forgive as the Lord has forgiven you. Over all these virtues put on love, which binds the rest together and makes them perfect. Christ's peace must reign in your hearts, since as members of the one body you have been called to that peace. Dedicate yourselves to thankfulness. Let the word of Christ, rich as it is, dwell in you. In wisdom made perfect, instruct and admonish one another. Sing gratefully to God from your hearts in psalms, hymns, and inspired songs. Whatever you do, whether in speech or in action, do it in

**the name of the Lord Jesus. Give thanks
to God the Father through him.**

This is another household code but some
distinctive Christian elements in human relationships are highlighted in it. In the wedding
liturgy, special emphasis might be placed on
the special need of forgiveness in love relationships. It is God's love and forgiveness of us
that is the reason for and the model of our
forgiveness of one another. The author urges
us to let the word of Christ dwell in us and to
speak with each other with the wisdom granted us by the Spirit. Communication on a regular, sustained basis is absolutely essential to
a healthy marriage; this might be mentioned
in the homily.

NT-7:   I Peter 3, 1-9

**You married women must obey your hus-
bands, so that any of them who do not
believe in the word of the gospel may be
won over apart from preaching, through
their wives' conduct. They have only to
observe the reverent purity of your way
of life. The affectation of an elaborate
hairdress, the wearing of golden jewelry,
or the donning of rich robes is not for
you. Your adornment is rather the hidden character of the heart, expressed in
the unfading beauty of a calm and gentle
disposition. This is precious in God's
eyes. The holy women of past ages used
to adorn themselves in this way, reliant
on God and obedient to their husbands
— for example, Sarah, who was subject
to Abraham and called him her master.
You are her children when you do what is
right and let no fears alarm you.
  You husbands, too, must show consideration for those who share your lives.**

Treat women with respect as the weaker sex, heirs just as much as you to the gracious gift of life. If you do so, nothing will keep your prayers from being answered.

In summary, then, all of you should be likeminded, sympathetic, loving toward one another, kindly disposed, and humble. Do not return evil for evil or insult for insult. Return a blessing instead. This you have been called to do, that you may receive a blessing as your inheritance.

The first part of this household code is directed to Christian women whose spouses are pagan. It suggests that by their conduct they might win over their husbands to the faith. There follows a diatribe against the use of cosmetics! If one can make allowance for the cultural setting of this reading which calls woman "the weaker sex" and extolls Sarah who called her husband her master, the reading does commend some important Christian virtues that every marriage relationship should take to heart, in particular, not returning wrong for wrong or anger for anger, but returning a blessing when one has been harmed. The successful marriage is one which seeks the truly good things in life: a forgiving atmosphere, peace in the home, fidelity, hospitality.

NT-8: I John 3, 18-24

Little children,
let us live in deed and in truth,
and not merely talk about it.
This is the way of knowing we are
    committed to the truth
and are at peace before him
no matter what our consciences may
    charge us with;

for God is greater than our hearts
and all is known to him.
Beloved,
if our consciences have nothing to charge
    us with,
we can be sure that God is with us
and that we will receive at his hands
whatever we ask.
Why? Because we are keeping his
    commandments
and doing what is pleasing in his sight.
His commandment is this:
we are to believe in the name of his Son,
    Jesus Christ,
and are to love one another as he
    commanded us.
Those who keep his commandments
    remain in him
and he in them.
And this is how we know that he remains
    in us:
from the Spirit that he gave us.

If we do what God commands, we will abide in God. Sometimes it is not an easy thing to know what are God's desires for us or for others. This reading addresses this situation and reminds us that even if we are uncertain as to how we stand before God, we should trust that God understands us better than we know ourselves. If we have faith in Jesus and try to love one another as God loves us, we should be confident that God will care for us. Couples will have to make many decisions, the rightness or wrongness of which may not always be clear. A well informed conscience, marked by honesty, by careful inquiry and by prayer, will guarantee peace of mind. But our love must not reside in words alone; it must issue in deeds.

NT-9: I John 4, 7-12

Beloved,
let us love one another
because love is of God;
everyone who loves is begotten of God
and has knowledge of God.
The man without love has known nothing
   of God,
for God is love.
God's love was revealed in our midst in this
   way:
he sent his only Son to the world
that we might have life through him.
Love, then, consists in this:
not that we have loved God,
but that he has loved us
and has sent his Son as an offering for
   our sins.
Beloved,
if God has loved us so,
we must have the same love for one
   another.
No one has ever seen God.
Yet if we love one another
God dwells in us,
and his love is brought to perfection in us.

The author can testify that the Christian community believes that God is love because they have seen and felt the Father's love in Jesus, his Son. Only the person who loves, the reading goes on to say, can truly know God because God is love. The invitation to love which marriage is, is an invitation to enter more deeply as time goes by into the mystery of your marriage partner and into the mystery that is God. It is the outpouring of God's love for us that brought us into being and enables us to live and love. Since we are made in God's image and likeness, we are called to imitate the love of God. Since God loved us first, we are called to love others first. We love others not because they love us, but because they are in themselves beautiful creations of our Father and worthy of our love as they are the objects of his.

NT-10:   Revelation 19, 1. 5-9

I, John, heard what sounded like the loud song of a great assembly in heaven. They were singing:
   "Alleluia!
   Salvation, glory, and might belong to our God."
   A voice coming from the throne cried out: "Praise our God, all you his servants, the small and the great, who revere him!" Then I heard what sounded like the shouts of a great crowd, of the roaring of the deep, or mighty peals of thunder, as they cried:
   "Alleluia!
The Lord is king,
   our God, the Almighty!
Let us rejoice and be glad,
   and give him glory!
For this is the wedding day of the Lamb,
   his bride has prepared herself for the wedding.
She has been given a dress to wear
   made of finest linen, brilliant white."
(The linen dress is the virtuous deeds of God's saints.)
   The angel then said to me: "Write this down: Happy are they who have been invited to the wedding feast of the Lamb."

The lamb is the symbol of Jesus in the book of Revelation. This passage is a hopeful and faith-filled look into the future of our world when it will be transformed into a kingdom of peace and justice. It is a song of joy at the nuptials between Christ and his bride, the church, at the end of time. Marriage can be and ought to be a foretaste, for the couple and for those who are touched by them, of that special time of union and peace. That is its prophetic character. Not only is marriage, therefore, a symbol of the mystical union *now* existing between Christ and his church, but it points to the final union between the Messiah and the redeemed. Some commentators attribute the custom of the bride wearing white to the white clothing of the saints who appear in the book of Revelation.

OPTIONS FOR THE GOSPEL

G-1:   Matthew 5, 1-12

When Jesus saw the crowds he went up on the mountainside. After he had sat down his disciples gathered around him, and he began to teach them:
   "How blest are the poor in spirit: the reign of God is theirs.
   Blest too are the sorrowing; they shall be consoled.
   (Blest are the lowly; they shall inherit the land.)
   Blest are they who hunger and thirst for holiness; they shall have their fill.
   Blest are they who show mercy; mercy shall be theirs.
   Blest are the single-hearted for they shall see God.
   Blest too are the peacemakers; they shall be called sons of God.
   Blest are those persecuted for holiness' sake; the reign of God is theirs.
   Blest are you when they insult you and persecute you and utter every kind of slander against you because of me.
   Be glad and rejoice, for your reward in heaven is great."

In the Gospel according to Matthew, the sermon containing the beatitudes is situated on a mountain, suggestive of Mount Sinai. The sermon is seen as the new law corresponding to the old law given to Moses. It spells out how a Christian should live in order to have joy and it is most appropriate advice for a married couple. It is not the self-satisfied, the materialistic person who will be blessed (and happy), but it is those who show mercy, who treat others gently, who endeavor to make peace, who are unencumbered in spirit and free to be loving who will be happy. Strengthening these habits within the marriage relationship enables the partners to radiate a Christian presence beyond their home. Those who are willing to pay the price that love of and commitment to another entails will be rewarded.

G-2:   Matthew 5, 13-16

Jesus said to his disciples: "You are the salt of the earth. But what if salt goes flat? How can you restore its flavor? Then it is good for nothing but to be thrown out and trampled underfoot.

"You are the light of the world. A city set on a hill cannot be hidden. Men do not light a lamp and then put it under a bushel basket. They set it on a stand where it gives light to all in the house. In the same way, your light must shine before men so that they may see your goodness in your acts and give praise to your heavenly Father."

Language note:
"People" could be substituted for "men" in the third sentence, and "all" could be used in place of "men" in the fifth sentence.

Jesus describes the nucleus of the future church as the salt of the earth, a city on a hill and a light to the world. On your wedding day, you are clearly the center of attraction, the city, the light that brightens the day and the salt that gives it flavor. You are called by God to continue to be salt, light and a beacon for others. That is achieved only by loving as Jesus loved us. The quality of a bride and groom can be felt on their wedding day by the way they are concerned for others, even on that special day honoring them. It is a good time to try to live that selfless love that will continue to make you a light for others throughout your life.

G-3:   Matthew 7, 21. 24-29

Jesus said to his disciples: "None of those who cry out, 'Lord, Lord,' will enter the kingdom of God but only the one who does the will of my Father in heaven.

"Anyone who hears my words and puts them into practice is like the wise man who built his house on rock. When the rainy season set in, the torrents came and the winds blew and buffeted his house. It did not collapse; it had been solidly set on rock. Anyone who hears my words but does not put them into practice is like the foolish man who built his house on sandy ground. The rains fell, the torrents came, the winds blew and lashed against his house. It collapsed under all this and was completely ruined."

Jesus finished this discourse and left the crowds spellbound at his teaching. The reason was that he taught with authority and not like the scribes.

(Short form: Matthew 7, 21. 24-25)

Jesus said to his disciples: "None of those who cry out 'Lord, Lord,' will enter the kingdom of God but only the one who does the will of my Father in heaven.

"Anyone who hears my words and puts them into practice is like the wise man who built his house on rock. When the rainy season set in, the torrents came and the winds blew and buffeted his

house. It did not collapse; it had been solidly set on rock."

You are about to build a life together in Christian marriage. Vows made on your wedding day have to be fulfilled through a thousand acts of fidelity, compassion and love. Marriage cannot be built on shifting sands but must be built on the rock of Christ and his teachings if it is to last. This part of the sermon on the Mount was directed to certain prophets and healers who were upsetting the church. The test of their work, it asserts, will not be their flashy achievements, but their obedience to the righteousness set forth in the sermon.

G-4:   Matthew 19, 3-6

Some Pharisees came up to Jesus and said, to test him, "May a man divorce his wife for any reason whatever?" He replied, "Have you not read that at the beginning the Creator made them male and female and declared, 'For this reason a man shall leave his father and mother and cling to his wife, and the two shall become as one'? Thus they are no longer two but one flesh. Therefore, let no man separate what God has joined."

The Pharisees are trying to trap Jesus into taking sides in a dispute about the interpretation of a section of the Torah (the law) dealing with divorce. The Torah said that a man could divorce his wife for "some unseemly thing." Naturally the argument revolved around what was meant by "some unseemly thing." One side claimed it meant adultery; the other claimed it meant anything that displeased the husband. Jesus, in answer, harkens back to the original order of creation. It was Moses who had permitted divorce as a concession to human weakness; Jesus, however, holds to the ideal that man and wife are joined together forever. The couple is called, assisted by God's grace in the sacrament of marriage, to be truly a foretaste of heavenly conditions — of fidelity beyond one's natural strength, of patience beyond one's own means. It is a prophetic vocation which deserves the support of friends and the Christian community.

G-5:   Matthew 22, 35-40

One of the Pharisees, a lawyer, in an attempt to trip up Jesus, asked him, "Teacher, which commandment of the law is the greatest?" Jesus said to him:
** "'You shall love the Lord your God**
** with your whole heart,**
** with your whole soul,**
** and with all your mind.'**
This is the greatest and first commandment. The second is like it:
** 'You shall love your neighbor as yourself.' On these two commandments the whole law is based, and the prophets as well."**

This summary of the law is also found in an earlier Jewish work called the Testaments of the Twelve Patriarchs, but Jesus links the two commandments in a new way. Love of God without love of neighbor is a deception; and love of neighbor without love of God can turn out to be self-love. There are three loves which make up the two essential commandments: love of God with your whole being, love and esteem of yourself as a precious creation of God, and love of neighbor equal to the love you have for yourself. To love in this manner poses a severe challenge to us; our world does not reward or commend those that live for others.

Self-centeredness (not the same as self-love) and looking out for number one seem to be rewarded. Married love can stand out like a beacon of hope in this dark world when it reaffirms the values of commitment, fidelity, generosity and compassion.

G-6:   Mark 10, 6-9

Jesus said: "At the beginning of creation God made them male and female; for this reason a man shall leave his father and mother and the two shall become as one. They are no longer two but one flesh. Therefore let no man separate what God has joined."

This is a Marcan parallel of G-4. The only difference between the two is that the Matthew setting is one of debate; the Mark setting is not. Consult the commentary on G-4.

G-7:   John 2, 1-11

There was a wedding at Cana in Galilee, and the mother of Jesus was there. Jesus and his disciples had likewise been invited to the celebration. At a certain point the wine ran out, and Jesus' mother told him, "They have no more wine." Jesus replied, "Woman, how does this concern of yours involve me? My hour has not yet come." His mother instructed those waiting on table, "Do whatever he tells you." As prescribed for Jewish ceremonial washings, there were at hand six stone jars, each one holding fifteen to twenty-five gallons. "Fill those

Pronunciation notes:
Cana = KAY - nuh
Galilee = GAL - i - lee

jars with water," Jesus ordered, at which they filled them to the brim. "Now," he said, "draw some out and take it to the waiter in charge." They did as he instructed them. The waiter in charge tasted the water made wine, without knowing where it had come from; only the waiters knew, since they had drawn the water. Then the waiter in charge called the groom over and remarked to him: "People usually serve the choice wine first; then when the guests have been drinking a while, a lesser vintage. What you have done is keep the choice wine until now." Jesus performed this first of his signs at Cana in Galilee. Thus did he reveal his glory, and his disciples believed in him.

This has been one of the most widely used texts in the Christian wedding liturgy since the Middle Ages. Jesus, who took upon himself our human flesh and condition, approves marriage by this gesture of compassion and love for the couple at Cana. The miracle is also a sign that God has broken into our history in a transforming way. Today, God promises to be with every couple in this sacrament of grace and power. Through the Spirit of Jesus granted to them, the clear, pure water of their lives together can be transformed into a fine wine, a cause of celebration for the Christian community.

G-8: John 15, 9-12

Jesus said to his disciples:
"As the Father has loved me,
so I have loved you.
Live on in my love.
You will live in my love
if you keep my commandments,
even as I have kept my Father's

commandments,
and live in his love.
And this I tell you
that my joy may be yours
and your joy may be complete.
This is my commandment:
love one another
as I have loved you."

G-9: John 15, 12-16

Jesus said to his disciples:
 "This is my commandment:
 love one another
 as I have loved you.
 There is no greater love than this:
 to lay down one's life for one's friends.
 You are my friends
 if you do what I command you.
 I no longer speak of you as slaves,
 for a slave does not know what his
   master is about.
 Instead, I call you friends,
 since I have made known to you all that
   I heard from my Father.
 It was not you who chose me,
 it was I who chose you
 to go forth and bear fruit.
 Your fruit must endure,
 so that all you ask the Father in my name
 he will give you."

Note: The commentary for G-8 and G-9 is the same and follows G-9.

(This commentary is for G-8 and G-9.) In giving up his life for us, Jesus set us an example of how to live and love. God wants us to be joyful; the way to that joy is obedience to God's commands, chief of which is the command to love one another as Jesus has loved us. Our relationship with God is not that of servant to master, but of child to parent, a child who is also called friend. We have been chosen to go forth and bear fruit. The fruit of this marriage will be the marriage itself and the love and progeny that will come from it. Ask the Father in Jesus' name so that your fruit may endure.

G-10:   John 17, 20-26

Jesus looked up to heaven and prayed:
"Holy Father,
I do not pray for my disciples alone.
I pray also for those who will believe in
  me through their word,
that all may be one
as you, Father, are in me, and I in you;
I pray that they may be (one) in us,
that the world may believe that you sent
  me.
I have given them the glory you gave me
that they may be one, as we are one —
I living in them, you living in me —
that their unity may be complete.
So shall the world know that you sent
  me,
and that you loved them as you loved me.
Father,
all those you gave me
I would have in my company
where I am,
to see this glory of mine
which is your gift to me,
because of the love you bore me before
  the world began.
Just Father,
the world has not known you,
but I have known you;
and these men have known that you sent
  me.
To them I have revealed your name,
and I will continue to reveal it
so that your love for me may live in them,
and I may live in them."

(Short form: John 17, 20-23)

Jesus looked up to heaven and prayed:
"Holy Father,
I do not pray for my disciples alone.
I pray also for those who believe in me
  through their word,
that all may be one
as you, Father, are in me, and I in you;
I pray that they may be (one) in us,

that the world may believe that you sent
    me.
I have given them the glory you gave me
that they may be one, as we are one —
I living in them, you living in me —
that their unity may be complete.
So shall the world know that you sent
    me,
and that you loved them as you loved
    me."

This reading is a love song by Christ to us.
He wants us to be as he is with the Father,
united in perfect union. The unity of Christians is to be a sign to the world that Jesus
was sent by God. Marriage in a preeminent
way is the sign of this love of God for the
world. Christians strive for this kind of union
but do it in a sinful world, conscious of our
deep need for God's grace to touch us and
transform us. That special grace is guaranteed
to the wedding couple in the sacrament of
marriage, not just on their wedding day, but
throughout their lives together.

CHAPTER FOUR

THE MUSIC FOR THE WEDDING LITURGY

We turn our attention now to one of the most creative and exciting elements of the wedding liturgy: the music. A well chosen program of music has the potential to draw people into the celebration and foster their participation in a way that words can never do. *Music in Catholic Worship*, a document prepared by the Catholic bishops of the United States in 1972, notes the important role that music plays in liturgy:

> Among the many signs and symbols used by the Church to celebrate its faith, music is of preeminent importance. As sacred song united to the words it forms an integral part of solemn liturgy. Yet the function of music is ministerial; it must serve and never dominate. Music should

assist the assembled believers to express and share the gift of faith that is within them and to nourish and strengthen their interior commitment of faith. It should heighten the texts so that they speak more fully and more effectively. The quality of joy and enthusiasm which music adds to community worship cannot be gained in any other way. It imparts a sense of unity to the gathered assembly and sets the appropriate tone for a particular celebration.

Music, in addition to expressing texts, can also unveil a dimension of meaning and feeling, a communication of ideas and intuitions which words alone cannot yield. This dimension is integral to the human personality and to our growth in faith. (Washington DC: United States Catholic Conference, 1972, nos. 23-24.)

The music at the wedding liturgy sets the tone for many levels of experience. It invites the assembly to participate with heart and mind and spirit. Music is not simply a "nice touch" to the liturgy, but indeed draws the whole person into a spirit of celebration. This can happen through music with words as well as through instrumental music. Usually, both kinds of music are used in the wedding liturgy.

The advice given at the end of Chapter One is worth reviewing as you begin to plan the music for the wedding liturgy. Three additional principles are offered here to assist in selecting music that will involve the assembly:

(1) **Appropriateness.** The music should be appropriate for a liturgical celebration. There are pastoral, liturgical and musical considerations which determine this. In particular, pay attention to the assembly when making musical decisions. The members of the assembly are not an audience; they are cele-

brators. Music is an expression of the assembly's prayer and praise to God for this wonderful occasion. For this reason, love songs that do not include God's love are inappropriate and better appreciated at the wedding reception which has its own special musical considerations. If you are considering certain favorite songs, the parish music minister can suggest which songs are appropriate to the wedding liturgy and which are more suited to other parts of the wedding celebration.

(2) **Readiness.** The assembly will best pray and sing with music they have sung before. Look for music, then, that is familiar to you and that you think your family and friends might know. With a little effort, you will be pleasantly surprised at how much music is accessible to you. For a start, look in the hymnals in your parish for a wealth of choices.

(3) **Graciousness.** Just as a hospitable greeting at the door of the church helps to make people feel welcome, so a gracious invitation to sing encourages participation and improves the quality of the singing. Ideally, a leader of song provides this service throughout the liturgy from the front of the church. If this is not possible, the priest or deacon could extend a personal invitation to the assembly to sing. It can be as simple as: "In order that everyone here might share in our rejoicing on this special day, let us together sing 'All Creatures of Our God and King' in one great voice of praise."

Finally, remember that music heightens the importance of whatever is spoken. When deciding what to sing, ask the following questions: (a) Why are we singing this particular piece of music at this time? and (b) Do we want to emphasize this moment of the liturgy through music? If these questions are answered unselfishly and with informed liturgical judgment,

FULFILLED IN YOUR HEARING

One of the most helpful ways to review possible music for the wedding liturgy is to actually hear it. In some parishes, the music minister has prepared a cassette tape of wedding music that he or she is proficient at playing and that the parish is familiar with. Ask if your musician has such a tape.

the music that you use will have a powerful effect on the liturgy. Using all of your favorite music doesn't guarantee a better or more festive celebration; it only guarantees a longer one.

WHAT SHALL WE SING?

Singing by the entire assembly at a wedding fully expresses the joy and unity of the celebrating community. It is not only appropriate, but encouraged. It allows people to participate in the liturgy with enthusiasm in a most unique way. There are many possibilities for singing in the wedding liturgy:

The Gathering Song. After the greeting by the presider at the beginning of the liturgy, an exuberant hymn of praise helps to gather the people together as a praying assembly. A gathering song is a perfect way to invite the assembly to respond to the stirring moment of the procession. A hymn here can truly be a paean of praise and thanksgiving for God's love freely showered on us all and personified in the liturgy by both of you as witnesses to that love.

The Responsorial Psalm. The assembly responds to the first reading with a very distinctive kind of song. There may be a wide variety of musical renditions, but the text is from that part of the Bible known as the Book of Psalms. The psalm at this point in the liturgy is a way for the assembly to acknowledge God's activity in humankind as proclaimed in the first reading. The words are those of our ancestors — those who have gone before us and have also framed their lives in God's love. The psalms have a message for everyone.

The assembly is seated during the responsorial psalm, usually eager to listen and respond. The leader of song sings the verses and assists the assembly with their easy antiphon, or refrain (indicated by "R"). The *Rite of*

Marriage recommends the following seven psalms, although others may be chosen (for example, Psalm 8 which is given after the first Old Testament reading in Chapter Three). Look for one that you feel expresses today's sentiments. There are a variety of musical settings for the psalms.

THE LANGUAGE OF THE PSALMS

The psalms that are printed here do not present any particular challenges to one's pronunciation skills, but other psalms that you may consider do. Ask the priest, deacon or music minister for assistance if you find any words that are difficult to pronounce.

Some suggestions are given in the margin here for alternative language that does not exclude women.

RP-1:   Psalm 33, 12. 18. 20-21. 22

R: The earth is full of the goodness of the Lord.

**Happy the nation whose God is the Lord,
the people he has chosen for his own inheritance.
But see, the eyes of the Lord are upon those who fear him,
upon those who hope for his kindness.**

R: The earth is full of the goodness of the Lord.

**Our soul waits for the Lord,
who is our help and our shield,
For in him our hearts rejoice;
in his holy name we trust.**

R: The earth is full of the goodness of the Lord.

**May your kindness, O Lord, be upon us
who have put our hope in you.**

R: The earth is full of the goodness of the Lord.

RP-2:   Psalm 34, 2-3. 4-5. 6-7. 8-9

R: I will bless the Lord at all times.

**I will bless the Lord at all times;
his praise shall be ever in my mouth.
Let my soul glory in the Lord;
the lowly will hear me and be glad.**

R: I will bless the Lord at all times.

**Glorify the Lord with me,
let us together extol his name.**

I sought the Lord, and he answered me
and delivered me from all my fears.

R: I will bless the Lord at all times.

Look to him that you may be radiant with
joy, and your faces may not blush with
shame.
When the afflicted man called out, the Lord
heard, and from all his distress he saved
him.

R: I will bless the Lord at all times.

The angel of the Lord encamps
around those who fear him, and delivers
them.
Taste and see how good the Lord is;
happy the man who takes refuge in him.

R: I will bless the Lord at all times.

Language note: "When the afflicted one called out" and "happy the one who takes refuge" could be substituted for "when the afflicted man called out" and "happy the man who takes refuge" in RP-2.

RP-3:   Psalm 103, 1-2. 8. 13. 17-18

R: The Lord is kind and merciful.

Bless the Lord, O my soul;
and all my being, bless his holy name.
Bless the Lord, O my soul,
and forget not all his benefits.

R: The Lord is kind and merciful.

Merciful and gracious is the Lord,
slow to anger and abounding in kindness.
As a father has compassion on his children,
so the Lord has compassion on those
who fear him.

R: The Lord is kind and merciful.

Language note: "As parents have compassion on their children" could be substituted for "as a father has compassion on his children" in RP-3.

But the kindness of the Lord is from
eternity to eternity toward those who
fear him,
And his justice toward children's children
among those who keep his covenant.

R: The Lord is kind and merciful.

RP-4:   Psalm 112, 1-2. 3-4. 5-7. 7-8. 9

R: Happy are those who do what the Lord
commands.

Happy the man who fears the Lord,
  who greatly delights in his commands.
His posterity shall be mighty upon the earth;
  the upright generation shall be blessed.

R: Happy are those who do what the Lord
  commands.

Wealth and riches shall be in his house;
  his generosity shall endure forever.
He dawns through the darkness, a light for
  the upright; he is gracious and merciful
  and just.

R: Happy are those who do what the Lord
  commands.

Well for the man who is gracious and lends,
  who conducts his affairs with justice;
He shall never be moved;
  the just man shall be in everlasting
  remembrance.

R: Happy are those who do what the Lord
  commands.

An evil report he shall not fear.
  His heart is firm, trusting in the Lord.
His heart is steadfast; he shall not fear
  till he looks down upon his foes.

R: Happy are those who do what the Lord
  commands.

Lavishly he gives to the poor;
  his generosity shall endure forever;
  his horn shall be exalted in glory.

R: Happy are those who do what the Lord
  commands.

RP-5:   Psalm 128, 1-2. 3. 4-5

R: Happy are those who fear the Lord.

Happy are you who fear the Lord,
  who walk in his ways!
For you shall eat the fruit of your
  handiwork; happy shall you be, and
  favored.

R: Happy are those who fear the Lord.

Language note: "Person" could be substituted for "man" in the first and third sections of RP-4. "She" and "her" could be used in a few places to balance the many times "he" and "his" are used.

Language note:
"Thus is the person blessed"
could be substituted for "thus is
the man blessed" in RP-5.

Your wife shall be like a fruitful vine
  in the recesses of your home;
Your children like olive plants
  around your table.

R: Happy are those who fear the Lord.

Behold, thus is the man blessed
  who fears the Lord.
The Lord bless you from Zion:
  may you see the prosperity of Jerusalem
  all the days of your life.

R: Happy are those who fear the Lord.

RP-6:   Psalm 145, 8-9. 10. 15. 17-18

R: The Lord is compassionate to all his
  creatures.

The Lord is gracious and merciful,
  slow to anger and of great kindness.
The Lord is good to all
  and compassionate toward all his works.

R: The Lord is compassionate to all his
  creatures.

Let all your works give you thanks, O Lord,
  and let your faithful ones bless you.
The eyes of all look hopefully to you,
  and you give them their food in due
  season.

R: The Lord is compassionate to all his
  creatures.

The Lord is just in all his ways
  and holy in all his works.
The Lord is near to all who call upon him,
  to all who call upon him in truth.

R: The Lord is compassionate to all his
  creatures.

RP-7:   Psalm 148, 1-2. 3-4. 9-10. 11-12. 12-14

R: Let all praise the name of the Lord.

Praise the Lord from the heavens,
  praise him in the heights;

Praise him, all you his angels,
praise him, all you his hosts.

R: Let all praise the name of the Lord.

Praise him, sun and moon;
praise him, all you shining stars.
Praise him, you highest heavens,
and your waters above the heavens.

R: Let all praise the name of the Lord.

You mountains and all you hills,
you fruit trees and all you cedars;
You wild beasts and all tame animals,
you creeping things and you winged fowl.

R: Let all praise the name of the Lord.

Let the kings of the earth and all peoples,
the princes and all the judges of the earth,
Young men too, and maidens,
old men and boys.

R: Let all praise the name of the Lord.

Praise the name of the Lord,
for his name alone is exalted;
His majesty is above earth and heaven,
and he has lifted up the horn of his people.

R: Let all praise the name of the Lord.

Language note:
"Old women and girls" could be added after "old men and boys" for balance in RP-7.

The Gospel Acclamation. The proclamation of the gospel is preceded by a joyful alleluia that prepares the assembly to hear the Good News. If the gospel acclamation is not sung, it is omitted. In this case, ask your musician, instead, to play an instrumental fanfare while the priest or deacon walks to the lectern.

The gospel acclamation may be done in a couple of different ways. The word "alleluia" may simply be sung repeatedly to a certain tune, or the leader of song may sing a particular verse which is preceded and followed by the assembly's singing of the alleluia refrain. If the second option is chosen, these are the verses that are suggested in the *Rite of Marriage*, although others are possible:

1. **God is love;
    let us love one another as he has loved us.**

2. **If we love one another,
    God will live in us in perfect love.**

3. **He who lives in love, lives in God,
    and God in him.**

4. **Everyone who loves is born of God and
    knows him.**

Language note:
"The one who lives in love" could be substituted for "he who lives in love" in selection #3 for the gospel acclamation verse.

During the season of Lent, a different refrain is used in place of the "alleluia" in the gospel acclamation. Your music minister may suggest several familiar options for this Lenten refrain.

The Marriage Rite. No music is necessary at this time with the exception of a bit of instrumental music while the wedding party moves into place. At the conclusion of the marriage rite, singing can release the feelings that are in the peoples' hearts. If the wedding is not taking place within a Mass (form II or III), the liturgy concludes soon after the marriage rite. In this case, the music might take the form of a departure song of praise. If the wedding is within a Mass (form I), consider using a brief musical selection during the procession of the gifts. Music at these places will be more effective than immediately after the blessing of rings.

(The next five sections relate to weddings within Mass only. If you will be using form II or III, skip down to the dismissal song.)

Preparation of the Gifts. Music here should not delay the liturgy. Therefore, instrumental music or a short vocal solo will function nicely during the preparation of gifts. Do not limit yourself to texts about bread, wine, wheat and grapes. Texts about praise, joy, love, and thanksgiving are all most acceptable.

The Eucharistic Acclamations. There are three acclamations during the eucharistic prayer: the "Holy, Holy" or "Sanctus," the

"Memorial Acclamation," and the "Great Amen" at the end of this prayer. These acclamations belong to the assembly. Ideally, they are sung so as to best express the unity of the assembly. Selecting familiar settings for these three acclamations is most important if this unity is to be achieved. Otherwise, music could actually interfere with participation in this situation. Your music minister can suggest settings that are commonly used in many parishes.

The Sign of Peace. The rite of peace is not a reception line. If people have greeted each other at the beginning of the liturgy, then this gesture can serve its intended purpose: to extend to each other a sign of Christ's peace. Singing is not recommended. Instrumental music may be played while a short exchange of peace takes place. As soon as possible, move to the breaking of the bread.

The Breaking of the Bread. Once the sign of peace is finished, the priest and communion ministers break the bread and pour the wine into the cups for communion. While this is taking place, the leader of song leads the assembly in singing the "Lamb of God." There are several familiar settings of this song which your music minister may suggest. Ideally, the song is repeated until the breaking of bread is finished.

Communion Song. The singing of songs together is an essential sign of our communion with God and with each other. A familiar hymn, a contemporary scriptural song or a psalm may be used during communion. Since people will be processing to communion, a refrain that they can sing without books or programs is suggested. After the initial refrain by the assembly, instrumental music or vocal solos are appropriate options. Depending on the size of the assembly, you may want to include several selections. The music here need not be reflective. The nature of these songs can reflect praise or thanksgiving, or God's love for humanity. The psalms suggested in the *Rite of Marriage* (see responsorial psalm section) are quite appropriate here as well.

Post-Communion or Dismissal Song. A final song of praise and rejoicing may be sung by the assembly either after communion or at the dismissal. When a festive instrumental recessional is used, a dismissal song is not necessary.

Finally on the topic of sung music, a reiteration of some advice from Chapter One: expressions of personal taste, such as your favorite song, can be effectively used at the wedding, but maybe not necessarily at the wedding liturgy. All of the events associated with your wedding — rehearsal dinner, liturgy, reception — offer distinct yet ample opportunities for you to imprint your personalities on this celebration. There are many dimensions to your love for each other. Make your impression on all the events. Liturgical music should express the gratitude and joy that you feel toward God for bringing you together. Use texts that include the Creator as part of your relationship. In the wedding liturgy, you offer your lives to each other and to God; in the words of the Second Vatican Council, you "stand before the world as a sign that God lives." Let the music of the liturgy reflect this.

INSTRUMENTAL MUSIC

Music that is sung by the assembly is primary in the wedding liturgy as in all liturgy. It is not the only type of appropriate music, however. Instrumental music can effectively complement the sung music and help to shape a beautiful, prayerful liturgy.

The Processional. The entrance procession is an inspirational highlight for the assembly.

It is a ceremonial movement that involves both bride and groom and liturgical ministers. It is a movement whereby representative members of the assembly express their willingness to go forward with the bride and groom in continued friendship, support and love. It is a symbolic action of movement into a new life. This is the reason why many parishes do not allow the composition popularly known as "Here Comes the Bride" to be played at weddings. Its very title limits the full meaning of the procession. Interestingly, this piece is losing its popularity in many circles. The *Trumpet Voluntary* attributed to Jeremiah Clarke has replaced "Here Comes the Bride" as one of the most popular festal processionals. (You may be familiar with the *Trumpet Voluntary* as the processional used at the wedding of Great Britain's Prince Charles and Lady Diana.)

There is an extensive repertoire of music for wedding processions. Confer with your music minister for advice. There are a number of recordings of commonly performed processionals available in stores, or your parish may have a tape (see "Fulfilled in Your Hearing" on page 96). Most organists are familiar with this music. The pieces are not very difficult to play and each one sounds terrific. Remember: a modest selection played well will have a far better effect on the liturgy than a rigorous selection poorly performed.

The Recessional. There are also many possible selections for the recessional. The tune commonly referred to as the "traditional wedding march" was composed by Felix Mendelssohn and is actually becoming less customary than one might suspect. Its usage on popular television programs and soap operas has considerably diminished its popularity at church weddings. It is being enthusiastically replaced by the *Trumpet Tune* of Henry Purcell and several other selections.

The Gathering. There is one other area of instrumental music that needs attention: the gathering of the assembly. The music used here is crucial in setting the tone for the liturgy. From the time that people enter the church, the music which they hear creates an atmosphere of either sobriety or festivity in their consciousness. They may not be aware of this effect of music on them, but nevertheless, it is happening. Slow, quiet music will tend to have a meditative effect, resulting in an inward and reflective assembly. This makes spontaneity and participation more difficult to achieve. Baroque music, in contrast for example, bubbles with an energy and enthusiasm that encourages and fosters gregariousness which, in turn, invites participation.

It is not necessary for you to know the exact titles of music for the gathering rite. The style can be contemporary or classical. Your music minister has the musical resources to assist the liturgical function of gathering. If the musician is limited in his or her repertoire, simply request cheerful music as people gather in the church.

As was mentioned in the Introduction to this book, many parishes and dioceses have established guidelines for the wedding liturgy, including the music. These policies were not created to confine you or limit your creativity. Rather, they were probably the result of abuses to the liturgy that would offend most people. Those who are regularly involved in preparing and celebrating weddings have been forced in the past to witness and even implement some outrageous and extravagant spectacles. The priest, deacon or music minister can probably tell you of some fascinating yet painful experiences with weddings.

Last but not least, do not delay in contacting the music minister and beginning the musical preparations for the wedding liturgy. Ideally, all the musical decisions should be finalized two weeks before the wedding. This will allow ample time for printing the program with the necessary musical information included. It will also contribute much to your peace of mind and that of the musician.

CHAPTER FIVE

THE ENVIRONMENT FOR THE WEDDING LITURGY

A wise person once said, "Tradition is the living faith of the dead; traditionalism is the dead faith of the living." This bit of wisdom deserves some consideration as you prepare the wedding liturgy. At every turn in the progression of this book, a gentle voice has raised an important question: in all your preparations, are you making sure that whatever is done at your wedding speaks an honest and full message of your love for each other and your regard for the people who will gather to celebrate and witness your marriage?

This book has also explored many of the signs, symbols, customs and rituals associated with weddings. Some of these elements help to tell the story of marriage today; others clearly are

WHAT IS ENVIRONMENT

At the beginning of Chapter Four, a document on music prepared by the Catholic bishops of the United States was quoted (*Music in Catholic Worship*). The bishops prepared a similar document in 1978 entitled *Environment and Art in Catholic Worship*. This document defines "environment" in this way:

By environment we mean the larger space in which the action of the assembly takes place. At its broadest, it is the setting of the building in its neighborhood, including outdoor spaces. More specifically it means the character of a particular space and how it affects the action of the assembly. There are elements in the environment, therefore, which contribute to the overall experience, e.g., the seating arrangement, the placement of liturgical centers of action, temporary decoration, light, acoustics, spaciousness, etc. The environment is appropriate when it is hospitable, when it clearly invites and needs an assembly of people to complete it. Furthermore, it is appropriate when it brings people close together so that they can see and hear the entire liturgical action, when it helps people feel involved and become involved. Such an environment works with the liturgy, not against it. (Washington DC: United States Catholic Conference, 1978, no. 24.)

outmoded or tell a story contrary to how you and others view marriage. That is why it is so important to search the tradition for what gives life and meaning for today. It is also important to discard those things which no longer express who we are as Christians in contemporary American culture. It takes an open mind and an honest heart to make these decisions. Avoid the persistent temptation to traditionalism. Avoid empty customs and theatrical rituals which express very little of your own best selves.

The temptation to traditionalism is probably nowhere more difficult to overcome than in creating an environment for the "perfect" wedding. Simply put, in our culture a great deal of money rides on keeping certain customs intact and an engaged couple overspending. However, you know from your own experience that when you are guests in someone's home, it is not the lavishness of the surroundings or the richness of the food that makes for a memorable occasion. Rather, what matters most is the care with which all is prepared and the attention given to you as guests. Hospitality is primary.

A simple rule of thumb is that you can't make up in glitter and extra flowers what you lack in genuine hospitality and graciousness. If you are preoccupied and fussing over the "things" of your wedding to the exclusion of the people, then everyone has been badly served. Therefore, these thoughts on environment for a wedding will stress three very basic themes:

ONE: Less is more.

TWO: Hospitality is a fundamental form of loving.

THREE: Spectacles are better left to Broadway, Las Vegas or Ringling Brothers.

Some practical considerations:

(1) People create the mood or environment for a wedding. Therefore, know yourself and do only what you know you can handle gracefully. A classic but often repeated situation is that of the bride who has an unrealistic notion of how she should look on the wedding day. She imagines herself floating down the aisle in a dress with a seventeen-foot train. What usually happens is that reality collides with the dream. The bride finds herself out-maneuvered by the train. She is either tripping over it herself or it is being stepped on by others. Every movement of the bride during the liturgy demands that someone in the wedding party must fuss over the train. In the end, yards of unnecessary cloth have become the center of attention. The women in your wedding end up being servants or ladies-in-waiting rather than the honored witnesses to the vows you are pronouncing.

(2) While the members of your wedding party are the chief witnesses to your vows, all who are in the assembly are witnesses in their own right. This should be reflected in the positioning of people. What often happens is that the wedding party gets all dressed up at great personal expense only to spend the entire liturgy with their less flattering side facing the greatest number of people. They become a well dressed wall between the assembly and the bride and groom. Graciousness demands that we do not turn our backs to people. In any other circumstances it would be considered very rude.

If there is space in your church, a more effective arrangement would be to have the wedding party stand or sit behind the altar or to the sides of it. In this way, they complete the circle of support around you as bride and groom (see diagram A, p. 112). It is also possible, if not preferable, to have them stand as couples. The best man and maid of honor stand at the top of the circle, but go to your sides for the exchange of vows and rings.

SANCTUARY DIAGRAMS

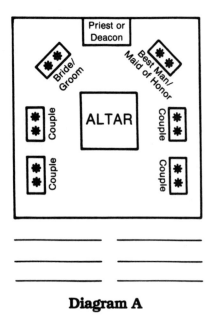

Diagram A

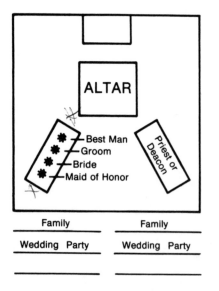

Diagram B

Another alternative, especially if the sanctuary space in your church is small, is to have the wedding party sit in the second row of the assembly, right behind your immediate families. The two of you, and perhaps the best man and maid of honor, sit in the sanctuary in such a way that you have eye contact with the assembly and with the priest or deacon (see diagram B). If the best man and maid of honor do not sit with you in the sanctuary throughout the liturgy, they simply come to your sides for the exchange of vows and rings.

Since it is the heart of the wedding liturgy, the exchange of vows and rings should be visible to the entire assembly. To do this most effectively, the two of you should stand in front of the altar facing the assembly with the best man and maid of honor to either side of you. The priest or deacon stands facing you, but slightly to the side so that his back is not to the assembly (see diagram C).

In some parishes, the bride and groom receive the gifts for the eucharist from their parents, godparents or other people important to them. The bride and groom then take the gifts to the altar and remain standing together as a couple near the altar for the rest of the liturgy. In this way, the importance of the couple as the main symbol of God's love is reinforced by their presence and visibility to the whole assembly.

(3) Furniture in the sanctuary should be limited to what is really necessary for the liturgy. If, for example, kneelers are not regularly used in your church's sanctuary, there is no reason to add them for the wedding liturgy. There is only one place in the liturgy when the assembly is directed to kneel — from the "Holy, Holy" to the "Great Amen" — and this only pertains to weddings within Mass. It is also the custom at many parishes that ministers who are in the sanctuary remain standing with the priest during the eucharistic prayer.

This would apply to the two of you and other members of the wedding party in the sanctuary. Excess furniture also tends to visibly clutter the sanctuary and obstruct the movement of those in the sanctuary.

(4) Flowers for a wedding are usually a major expense and, yet, they are often placed in such a way that they have little visual effect or they become a real distraction or obstacle to visibility. If, for example, flowers are placed on the floor near the altar, they are often too low to be seen by the majority of the assembly, especially if the wedding party stands in front of them. In some cases, the flower arrangements are well done but placed on poorly designed stands or in ways which compete with the placement of the people in the sanctuary. Here it would be important to work with a florist who knows what is best for the particular church, rather than purchasing generic "one-size-fits-all" arrangements.

There are many alternatives to the customary floral arrangements seen at weddings. Some couples simply choose to gather flowers of the season from the gardens of family and friends. Other couples put their money into flowering or green plants that can provide a beautiful setting at the wedding and then can be planted or used in their home as a reminder of the wedding. Flowers can also be used in places other than the sanctuary, particularly at the entrance or gathering space of the church, thus making a gracious sign of welcome to people as they arrive. The impact of flowers at the entrance is often much greater than an arrangement lost in an already crowded sanctuary. It is a courtesy to leave the flowers at the church after the wedding for the whole parish to enjoy.

It is also important to remember that many parishes have a committee of people who work throughout the year at creating a worship environment which will reflect the unfolding of

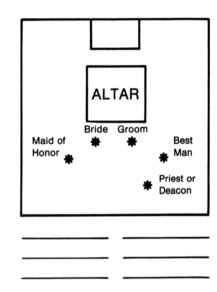

Diagram C

the various liturgical seasons. They might use banners or plants, flowers, found objects or empty spaces to express Lent, Easter, Advent, Christmas or Pentecost. These various seasonal decorations for the parish have priority over things brought in for weddings. It is a good idea to check with the local parish to see what, if any, decorations will be in place at the time of your wedding. Then, you can determine what flowers might be appropriate for the occasion. In some cases, the parish decorations are quite substantial and beautiful and you may not need any additional flowers.

Finally, if other weddings are scheduled in the church on the same day, you might consider getting together with the other couples and purchasing the flowers together. This can significantly reduce the cost for each couple. The parish can provide you with the names and phone numbers of other couples whose weddings are scheduled for the same day.

(5) An item related to flowers is the aisle runner. This is an unnecessary nuisance that prompts empty and often ridiculous looking ceremony for unrolling it. More and more, the aisle runners are being made of plastic rather than cloth. When this type of runner is placed on top of carpet, a significant safety hazard is created. As people are leaving the church or going to communion, they will have to walk on the runner. Some people could easily lose their footing or trip on the runner/carpet combination. (This is true even of cloth runners.) Hospitality demands consideration for those who might have difficulty walking on this surface. All in all, aisle runners are best avoided altogether.

(6) One of the consistent suggestions in this book has been to avoid adding ceremonies and prayers to the wedding liturgy and, instead, to prepare and celebrate the given options well. One such additional ceremony that you may have seen at weddings involves the lighting of

a special "unity" or "marriage" candle after the exchange of vows and rings. Often, this candle is placed on the altar and surrounded by flowers. If you do decide to use this additional ceremony in the wedding liturgy, it is important to place the candle in such a way that it does not dominate the altar or distract from the importance of the eucharist and the people in the sanctuary. A better arrangement is to place the candle on another table or stand elsewhere in the sanctuary, thus allowing the altar to serve its primary function as the table for the eucharistic meal.

(7) At important moments like a wedding, the honesty and integrity with which you present yourselves to one another, family and friends is critical. It is a time to open your hearts before God and to invite all to witness and support the sincerity of your commitment. In light of this, anything in the environment which is artificial (even silk flowers) becomes a sign contrary to what you wish to express.

Above all, remember that the beauty of the day and the mood which is created ultimately comes through you and how you choose to express your happiness. Be honest, be simple, be hospitable.

SAMPLE WEDDING PROGRAMS

The program, or order of service, for the wedding liturgy need not be fancy or elaborate. A simple, well designed program can be an attractive reminder of your wedding, while serving primarily to provide the texts and subtle directions needed by the assembly. If there is an artist among your relatives or friends, you might ask that person to design a cover or do calligraphy. Before printing the program, make sure that you have finalized the choices of prayers, readings and music with the priest or deacon and the music minister.

Three sample formats are provided here. In the first, the assembly is being invited to sing a number of times, and the notes indicate where the music would be reprinted. Less music is used in the second format, and certain prayers from the wedding liturgy have been reprinted to encourage the assembly to participate in saying them. This is suggested if you are expecting a large number of non-Catholics who would otherwise not know these prayers. The third format is like the second, but for a wedding outside of Mass (forms II and III). Your parish may also have a format of its own; check with the parish.

Sample Program #1

The Wedding of
Sarah Ann Johnson and Don Howard Giannella

Reverend James Thompson, presiding

Saturday, June 27, 1987
Saint Benedict Church, Hockessin, Delaware

*   *   *   *   *

PROCESSION (stand)   *St. Anthony Chorale*   Brahms
                                       (from Variations on a Theme by Haydn)

GREETING

GATHERING SONG   *All Creatures of Our God and King*
                                       [reprint words and, if possible, music
                                       here]

OPENING PRAYER

FIRST READING (sit)   Genesis 1, 26-28. 31
                                       Joe Niegoski, reader

RESPONSE   *O Lord, How Wonderful
                                       Your Name*   Olawski
                                       (based on Psalm 8)
                                       [reprint refrain, including music, here]

SECOND READING   Colossians 3, 12-17
                                       Ann McDonald, reader

GOSPEL ACCLAMATION (stand)   *Alleluia*

GOSPEL   Matthew 5, 13-16

HOMILY (sit)

CONSENT AND EXCHANGE OF VOWS

BLESSING AND EXCHANGE OF RINGS

GENERAL INTERCESSIONS   Response: Lord, hear our prayer.

PREPARATION OF THE GIFTS

HOLY, HOLY   (from *A Community Mass*)   Proulx
[reprint words and music here]

MEMORIAL ACCLAMATION   (from *A Community Mass*)   Proulx
[reprint words and music here]

GREAT AMEN

THE LORD'S PRAYER (stand)

THE NUPTIAL BLESSING

SIGN OF PEACE

THE BREAKING OF BREAD   *Lamb of God*   Parker
[reprint words and music here]

COMMUNION (sit)

POST-COMMUNION   *I Have Loved You*   Joncas
[reprint refrain, including music, here]

BLESSING (stand)

RECESSIONAL   *Rigaudon*   Campra

*   *   *   *   *

Holy Angels Parish
celebrates the wedding of
Arthur Sean Moore and Maria Kathleen O'Connor

Reverend William Kowalski, presiding

Saturday, October 24, 1988

*   *   *   *   *

PROCESSION (stand)	*Trumpet Tune*	Purcell

GREETING

OPENING PRAYER

FIRST READING (sit)
Song of Songs 2, 8-10. 14. 16; 8, 6-7
Laura Maguire, reader
Response: Thanks be to God.

RESPONSORIAL PSALM
Psalm 33, 12. 18. 20-21. 22
Response: The earth is full of the
                        goodness of the Lord.

SECOND READING
I Corinthians 12, 31—13, 8
Anthony Tomasi, reader
Response: Thanks be to God.

GOSPEL ACCLAMATION (stand)
Alleluia

GOSPEL
John 15, 9-12
Response: Praise to you, Lord Jesus
                        Christ.

HOMILY (sit)

CONSENT AND EXCHANGE OF VOWS

BLESSING AND EXCHANGE OF RINGS

GENERAL INTERCESSIONS
Response: Lord, hear our prayer.

PREPARATION OF THE GIFTS

HOLY, HOLY	Holy, holy, holy Lord, God of power and might, heaven and earth are full of your glory. Hosanna in the highest. Blessed is he who comes in the name of the Lord. Hosanna in the highest.
MEMORIAL ACCLAMATION	When we eat this bread and drink this cup, we proclaim your death, Lord Jesus, until you come in glory.
GREAT AMEN	
THE LORD'S PRAYER (stand)	Our Father, who art in heaven, hallowed be thy name; thy kingdom come; thy will be done on earth as it is in heaven. Give us this day our daily bread; and forgive us our trespasses as we forgive those who trespass against us; and lead us not into temptation, but deliver us from evil.
THE NUPTIAL BLESSING	
SIGN OF PEACE	
THE BREAKING OF BREAD	Lamb of God, you take away the sins of the world: have mercy on us. Lamb of God, you take away the sins of the world: have mercy on us. Lamb of God, you take away the sins of the world: grant us peace.
COMMUNION (sit)	
SONG OF PRAISE	*Joyful, Joyful* *We Adore Thee* Beethoven [reprint words and music here]

FINAL BLESSING (Please stand and extend your right arm toward Arthur and Maria, and join Father Kowalski in this blessing of the couple:)

May almighty God, with his Word of blessing, unite your hearts in the never-ending bond of pure love.

May your children bring you happiness, and may your generous love for them be returned to you, many times over.

May the peace of Christ live always in your hearts and in your home.

May you have true friends to stand by you, both in joy and in sorrow.

May you be ready and willing to help and comfort all who come to you in need.

And may the blessings promised to the compassionate be yours in abundance.

May you find happiness and satisfaction in your work. May daily problems never cause you undue anxiety, nor the desire for earthly possessions dominate your lives. But may your hearts' first desire be always the good things waiting for you in the life of heaven.

May the Lord bless you with many happy years together, so that you may enjoy the rewards of a good life. And after you have served him loyally in his kingdom on earth, may he welcome you to his eternal kingdom in heaven.

RECESSIONAL   *Rondeau*   Mouret

*   *   *   *   *

Sample Program #3

Holy Angels Parish
celebrates the wedding of
Arthur Sean Moore and Maria Kathleen O'Connor

Reverend William Kowalski, Holy Angels Church
Reverend Barbara Ferguson, Christ Episcopal Church
clergy

Saturday, October 24, 1988

*   *   *   *   *

PROCESSION (stand)	*Trumpet Tune*	Purcell

GREETING

OPENING PRAYER

FIRST READING (sit)
Song of Songs 2, 8-10. 14. 16; 8, 6-7
Laura Maguire, reader
Response: Thanks be to God.

RESPONSORIAL PSALM
Psalm 33, 12. 18. 20-21. 22
Response: The earth is full of the
goodness of the Lord.

SECOND READING
I Corinthians 12, 31—13, 8
Anthony Tomasi, reader
Response: Thanks be to God.

GOSPEL ACCLAMATION (stand)   *Alleluia*

GOSPEL
John 15, 9-12
Response: Praise to you, Lord Jesus
Christ.

HOMILY (sit)

CONSENT AND EXCHANGE OF VOWS

BLESSING AND EXCHANGE OF RINGS

GENERAL INTERCESSIONS   Response: Lord, hear our prayer.

NUPTIAL BLESSING

SONG OF PRAISE   *Joyful, Joyful*
                                      We Adore Thee   Beethoven

                                      [reprint words and music here]

THE LORD'S PRAYER   Our Father, who art in heaven,
                                      hallowed by thy name;
                                      thy kingdom come;
                                      thy will be done on earth as it is in
                                          heaven.
                                      Give us this day our daily bread;
                                      and forgive us our trespasses
                                      as we forgive those who trespass
                                          against us;
                                      and lead us not into temptation,
                                      but deliver us from evil.
                                      For thine is the kingdom, and the power,
                                      and the glory, for ever and ever. Amen.

FINAL BLESSING   (Please extend your right arm toward Arthur and Maria, and
    join Father Kowalski in this blessing of the couple:)

    May almighty God, with his Word of blessing, unite your hearts in the
        never-ending bond of pure love.
    May your children bring you happiness, and may your generous love for
        them be returned to you, many times over.
    May the peace of Christ live always in your hearts and in your home.
    May you have true friends to stand by you, both in joy and in sorrow.
    May you be ready and willing to help and comfort all who come to you
        in need.
    And may the blessings promised to the compassionate be yours in
        abundance.
    May you find happiness and satisfaction in your work. May daily problems
        never cause you undue anxiety, nor the desire for earthly possessions
        dominate your lives. But may your hearts' first desire be always the good
        things waiting for you in the life of heaven.
    May the Lord bless you with many happy years together, so that you may
        enjoy the rewards of a good life. And after you have served him loyally
        in his kingdom on earth, may he welcome you to his eternal kingdom
        in heaven.

RECESSIONAL   *Rondeau*   Mouret

                    *   *   *   *   *

SAMPLE GENERAL INTERCESSIONS

Sample Intercessions #1

Presider: The Lord is here among us: in the Word proclaimed to us, in the exchange of vows by N. and N., and in our very assembly. Let us present to the Lord our prayers for the needs of the church and of the world.

Reader: For the communion of all Christian churches, that all who follow Christ may live in the unity for which Christ prayed, let us pray to the Lord.

All: Lord, hear our prayer.

Reader: For the parishes of which N. and N. have been a part: (here name the churches where you were baptized, where you celebrated First Communion and Confirmation, and other parishes or college chapel communities of which you have been a part), let us pray to the Lord.

All: Lord, hear our prayer.

Reader: For our nation and this city, and for those who serve in our government, let us pray to the Lord.

All: Lord, hear our prayer.

Reader: For the poor, the homeless, and the unemployed of this city, and for all who suffer under persecution, let us pray to the Lord.

All: Lord, hear our prayer.

Reader: For the parents and families of N. and N., for their godparents (here name your godparents), and for all who formed them in faith, let us pray to the Lord.

All: Lord, hear our prayer.

Reader: For the deceased relatives of N. and N., for the sick and for those who will be travelling from here, let us pray to the Lord.

All: Lord, hear our prayer.

Reader: For our personal intentions, let us pray in silence.

(Pause)

Presider: Lord, hear the prayers that this church offers today. Grant them as may be best for us and for the building up of your kingdom of justice and peace. We ask this through Christ our Lord.

All: Amen.

Sample Intercessions #2

Presider: Let us pray:

Reader: For the Church throughout the world and for those who serve the Church, that all the People of God might preach and practice the gospel of Christ, we pray to the Lord.

All: Lord, hear our prayer.

Reader: For the Jewish people, the first to hear the word of God, that they may continue to grow in the love of God's name and in faithfulness to the covenant, we pray to the Lord.

All: Lord, hear our prayer. *T. F. L.*

Reader: For the outcasts and the downtrodden of our city and our nation, that they may find refuge and compassion in our churches and families, we pray to the Lord.

All: Lord, hear our prayer.

Reader: For family members who have gone before us marked with the sign of faith, especially (mention here deceased relatives), that our prayer today may be joined with theirs, we pray to the Lord.

All: Lord, hear our prayer.

Reader: For the families and friends of N. and N. gathered here today and those unable to be with us, that we may support one another in times of need as we rejoice with one another today, we pray to the Lord.

All: Lord, hear our prayer.

Reader: For N. and N., that the Lord bless them with many happy years together, we pray to the Lord.

All: Lord, hear our prayer.

Reader: For the intentions that each of us offers today, we pray in silence.

(Pause)

Presider: Lord, in the joy of this celebration, we offer these prayers for the Church and the world. We graciously ask you to fulfill our needs and guide our own actions so as to build up your kingdom. We ask this through Christ our Lord.

All: Amen.

CELEBRATING MARRIAGE

Planning Sheet

Church: _____   Date and Time: _____

Rehearsal Date and Time: _____

The People in The Wedding Liturgy

Bride: _____   Groom: _____

Presider (Priest or Deacon): _____

Witnesses (Best Man, Maid of Honor): _____

Musicians: Organist: _____
          Leader of Song: _____
          Others: _____

Readers: First Reading: _____
       Second Reading: _____
       General Intercessions: _____

Communion Ministers: _____
_____

Ushers/Bridesmaids: _____
_____

Altar Servers: _____

Others: _____

The Order of the Wedding Liturgy

Form to be used: _____ I. The Rite for Celebrating Marriage During Mass

_____ II. The Rite for Celebrating Marriage Outside Mass

_____ III. The Rite for Celebrating Marriage Between a Catholic and an Unbaptized Person

Gathering of the Assembly (page 26) _____

_____

Procession (page 28) _____

_____

Seating Diagram

Since the floor plan of each church is different, use the space below to draw a diagram indicating where the couple and others will sit:

Gathering and Entrance Rites

Greeting (pages 29-30)	1	2	3						
Penitential Rite (pages 30-32)	1	2	3						
Opening Prayer (pages 32-34)	1	2	3	4					

Liturgy of the Word

First Reading (pages 59-70)	1	2	3	4	5	6	7	8	
Responsorial Psalm (pages 97-101)	1	2	3	4	5	6	7		
Second Reading (pages 70-82)	1	2	3	4	5	6	7	8	9	10
Gospel Acclamation (page 101)	1	2	3	4					
Gospel (pages 82-91)	1	2	3	4	5	6	7	8	9	10

Marriage Rite

Exchange of Vows (pages 36-37)	1	2	3	4
Blessing of Rings (pages 37-38)	1	2	3	

General Intercessions to be prepared by: _____

Liturgy of the Eucharist

Gifts brought forward by: _____

Prayer over Gifts (pages 40-41)	1	2	3	
Preface (pages 41-43)	1	2	3	
Memorial Acclamation (page 44)	1	2	3	4
Nuptial Blessing (pages 45-49)	1	2	3	
Communion (page 50)	Bread and Wine		Bread only	
Prayer after Communion (pages 51-52)	1	2	3	

Concluding Rites

Final Blessing (pages 52-54)	1	2	3	4
Dismissal (page 55)	1	2	3	

Musical Selections

†Processional: _____ Only a Shadow _____

Gathering Song: _____

Responsorial Psalm: _____

Gospel Acclamation: _____

Preparation of the Gifts: _____

Holy, Holy: _____

Memorial Acclamation: _____

Great Amen: _____

Our Father

Lamb of God: _____

Communion: _____ Come to the Water _____

† Post-Communion or Dismissal Song: _Bind Us Together_

Recessional: _____

Other Music: _____

_____

_____

About the Authors

Paul Covino is the Associate Director of the Georgetown Center for Liturgy, Spirituality and the Arts, and teaches in the Certificate Program in Liturgical Studies at Georgetown University. He directs a wedding liturgy preparation program for engaged couples at Holy Trinity Parish in Washington, DC, where he has also served as liturgy coordinator.

Lawrence Madden, S.J., is the founder and Director of The Georgetown Center for Liturgy, Spirituality and the Arts. He is Adjunct Professor of Preaching and Liturgical Celebration at the Washington Theological Union, and Associate Pastor of Holy Trinity Parish.

Elaine Rendler is a faculty member at Georgetown University, teaching in both the Department of Fine Arts and the Georgetown Center for Liturgy, Spirituality and the Arts. She is the Director of the Certificate Program in Liturgical Studies at Georgetown University and has led workshops in liturgy and music throughout the country.

John Buscemi, a priest of the Diocese of Madison, Wisconsin, is an artist, a liturgist, a consultant to church building and renovation projects, and teaches at the Institute for Pastoral Studies, Loyola University, Chicago. He is currently in residence at St. Mary's Church, Janesville, Wisconsin, where he has also served as associate pastor.

The Georgetown Center for Liturgy, Spirituality and the Arts is a jointly sponsored project of Georgetown University and Holy Trinity Church in Washington DC. Through its various workshops, courses, and publications, the Center strives to assist American parishes in the continuing work of liturgical renewal.